DK EYEWITNESS TRAVEL

TOP
SINGAPORE

JENNIFER EVELAND
SUSY ATKINSON

Top 10 Singapore Highlights

The Top 10 of Everything

CONTENTS

Singapore Area by Area

Streetsmart

Within each Top 10 list in this book, no hierarchy of quality or popularity is implied. All 10 are, in the editor's opinion, of roughly equal merit.
   Throughout this book, floors are referred to in accordance with American usage; i.e., the "first floor" is at ground level.

Front cover and spine Singapore City, Marina Bay Sands and Gardens by the Bay trees
Back cover Night view of the Buddha Tooth Relic Temple in Singapore Chinatown
Title page Sri Veeramakaliamman Temple

The information in this DK Eyewitness Top 10 Travel Guide is checked regularly. Every effort has been made to ensure that this book is as up-to-date as possible at the time of going to press. Some details, however, such as telephone numbers, opening hours, prices, gallery hanging arrangements and travel information are liable to change. The publishers cannot accept responsibility for any consequences arising from the use of this book, nor for any material on third-party websites, and cannot guarantee that any website address in this book will be a suitable source of travel information. We value the views and suggestions of our readers very highly. Please write to: Publisher, DK Eyewitness Travel Guides, Dorling Kindersley, 80 Strand, London WC2R 0RL, Great Britain, or email travelguides@dk.com

Welcome to
Singapore

Lion city. Major Asian powerhouse. Cultural melting pot. Shopping mecca. Fusion-food heaven. An island city-state of gleaming skyscrapers and primary rainforest, the Republic of Singapore contrasts striking modernity with its traditional heritage like nowhere else. With Eyewitness Top 10 Singapore, it's yours to explore.

Small and densely populated, this tropical city-state is constantly reinventing itself. The space-age **Gardens by the Bay**, part natural wonder, part epic fantasy land, face the downtown urban jungle. While looking to the future, Singapore embraces its past. Its colonial legacy is preserved in magnificent buildings housing the **National Gallery** and the **Asian Civilisation Museum**. Poignant memories of **World War II** are scattered across the island, while colorful pre-war shophouses have been reborn as hip boutiques and cafés.

Singapore is full of surprises: Taoist and Hindu temples, Muslim mosques, and Christian churches share streets with sublime spas and chic rooftop bars. Whether you are eyeing designer goods in the luxury malls of **Orchard Road**, weaving through stalls in **Chinatown**, sipping a Singapore Sling in **Raffles Hotel**, or slurping a fiery laksa in an open-air hawker centre, there is never enough time for everything on offer. With eye-catching festivals and events, from **Chinese New Year** to the Singapore Grand Prix, it's all here.

Whether you're coming for a weekend or a week, our Top 10 guide brings together the best of everything Singapore has to offer, from the bright lights of **Marina Bay** to the boisterous laneways of **Little India**. The guide gives you tips throughout, from seeking out what's free to avoiding the crowds, plus seven easy-to-follow itineraries, designed to help you visit a clutch of sights in a short space of time. Add inspiring photography and detailed maps, and you have the essential travel companion. **Enjoy the book, and enjoy Singapore.**

Clockwise from top: **Thian Hock Keng Temple, ION Orchard mall on Orchard Road, Gardens by the Bay, the Marina Bay skyline, Chinese New Year celebrations, Raffles Hotel, Canning Park**

Exploring Singapore

For sights to see and cultures to experience, visitors to Singapore are spoiled for choice. Whether you have a couple of days' stopover between flights or have come to get a fuller flavor of this Asian city-state, here are some ideas for two and four days of sightseeing in Singapore.

Key
— Two day itinerary
— Four day itinerary

Orchard Road is home to a number of luxury malls, such as Paragon

Two Days in Singapore

Day ❶

MORNING

Absorb the colonial atmosphere over breakfast at **Raffles Hotel** (see pp30–31) before visiting the **National Museum of Singapore** (see pp12–13) for an hour or two. Take in luxury malls on **Orchard Road** (see pp94–9) or check out the **Singapore Botanic Gardens** (see pp24–5).

AFTERNOON

Immerse yourself in Chinatown, visit **Thian Hock Keng Temple** (see pp16–17), then stroll (or take a bumboat) along the **Singapore River** (see pp14–15). Explore **Gardens by the Bay** (see pp28–9), have a sunset drink atop **Marina Bay Sands** (see p28) and circle the lit-up bay at night.

Day ❷

MORNING

Begin by exploring the colorful lanes of **Little India and Kampong Glam**

(see pp78–85). Admire the **Sri Veeramakaliamman Temple** (see pp20–21) and **Sultan Mosque** (see pp18–19), and try local food in a hawker centre (see pp60–61).

AFTERNOON

Depending on your interests, head to the beaches and attractions on **Sentosa** island (see pp32–3) or spend the afternoon at the vast **Singapore Zoo**, taking in the unique **River Safari** and **Night Safari** (see pp26–7).

Sentosa Island provides a tranquil getaway from the bustle of the city

Sri Veeramakaliamman
Temple

Kampong
Glam

Little India   Sultan Mosque

Colonial District

Raffles Hotel

Raffles
Boulevard

Joo Chiat
3 miles (5 km)

Esplanade-
Theatres on
the Bay

Singapore
Flyer

Marina Bay Sands

Gardens by
the Bay

Clarke Quay is a great spot for a
riverside evening drink

Day ❷
MORNING
Check out the Colonial District's
architecture, potter around **Raffles
Hotel** (see pp30–31) and see
Southeast Asian masterpieces in the
National Gallery Singapore (see p38).
AFTERNOON
Dip into **Katong/Joo Chiat** (see p104)
for Peranakan food and architecture,
before shopping in Bugis or along
Raffles Boulevard. After a "flight" on
the **Singapore Flyer**, close out the
day at **Marina Bay** (see pp28–9).

Day ❸
MORNING
Begin early to enjoy either fun-filled
Sentosa (see pp32–3) or a trip to
Pulau Ubin (see p103) to experience
old rural Singapore.
AFTERNOON
Take a stroll along the stunning
Southern Ridges (see p100) before
hitting charming **Dempsey Road** (see
p104) for dinner and cocktails.

Day ❹
MORNING
Start off with a morning turn in
Kampong Glam for boutiques and
brunch, then explore **Little India**'s
Hindu temples (see pp78–81). Hit up
the malls on **Orchard Road** (see
pp94–9), finishing at the **National
Orchid Garden** in the **Singapore
Botanic Gardens** (see pp24–5).
AFTERNOON
Head down to **Gardens by the Bay**
(see pp28–9) and spend an afternoon
cooling down in the domed Cloud
Forest. Come evening, return east
to catch a live show at **Marina Bay
Sands** (see p28) or **Esplanade –
Theatres on the Bay** (see p64).

Singapore Zoo is home to some local
and not-so-local species of animal

Four Days in Singapore

Day ❶
MORNING
Visit **Thian Hock Keng Temple** (see
pp16–17) and **Chinatown**'s authentic
shops (see p76). Next, spend a couple
of hours in the **National Museum of
Singapore** (see pp12–13).
AFTERNOON
Head north to **Singapore Zoo** (see
pp26–7), where primates swing
overhead. Take the **Night Safari**
before enjoying late-night drinks at
lively Boat Quay or Clarke Quay on
the **Singapore River** (see pp14–15).

Top 10 Singapore Highlights

The otherworldly Supertree Grove
at Gardens by the Bay, Marina Bay

🔟 Singapore Highlights

At the crossroads of east and west, Singapore has a complex mix of culture and history. The grand Neo-Classical buildings of the Colonial District stand alongside the ethnically diverse neighborhoods of Chinatown, Little India, and Kampong Glam, with the Singapore River carving its way between them. It is a multifaceted city with both traditional and modern appeal.

National Museum of Singapore

The ideal introduction to Singapore and its cultural influences, the refurbished museum presents history using multimedia displays *(see pp12–13)*.

Singapore River

The Singapore River is lined by dining and leisure establishments. It is best experienced aboard a restored bumboat *(see pp14–15)*.

Thian Hock Keng Temple

This is Singapore's first Chinese Taoist temple and one of its finest. It is a good starting point for exploring Chinatown *(see pp16–18)*.

Sultan Mosque

With its gold onion domes that rise above Kampong Glam, the city's traditional Muslim quarter, Sultan Mosque is a fine blend of Persian, Moorish, and Turkish design *(see pp18–19)*.

Sri Veeramakaliamman Temple

Statues of Hindu gods crowd this temple's roof, watching over Little India. Dedicated to the goddess Kali, this temple is one of Singapore's oldest *(see pp20–21)*.

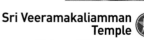

0 meters 800
0 yards 800

Singapore Botanic Gardens 6

On sprawling grounds just beyond the city center, the beautifully maintained Singapore Botanic Gardens are especially refreshing in the early mornings, when the air is a little cooler *(see pp24–5)*.

7 Singapore Zoo, Night Safari, and River Safari

A perennial tourist favorite, this award-winning zoo is recommended for all. The Night Safari is the world's first for viewing nocturnal animals in a natural habitat *(see pp26–7)*.

Marina Bay 8

Surrounded by iconic Singapore sights such as the Merlion, Marina Bay Sands, and the Singapore Flyer, the bay's skyline is breathtaking both day and night *(see pp28–9)*.

9 Raffles Hotel

This grand hotel represents the enduring romance of colonial exploration that helped to build early Singapore, and the drive for absolute luxury that characterizes its success *(see pp30–31)*.

Sentosa 10

Singapore's popular playground, Sentosa is an island of relaxing spas and resorts, thrilling water and land sports, and other attractions *(see pp32–3)*.

TOP 10 ⭐ National Museum of Singapore

The colonial splendor of the National Museum, unveiled on Queen Victoria's Golden Jubilee in 1887, reflects the British empire at its most confident. Following Singapore's independence in 1965, the building was developed as a monument to the country's history and culture. The rear of the museum is a modern wing, its glass and steel offering a striking contrast to the original, restored building. Singapore's story is told largely using interactive exhibits.

4 The Glass Passage
The construction of the glass passage is an architectural achievement and a visually stunning link between old and new.

5 Surviving Syonan
This exhibition looks at the ways Singapore's people responded to the harsh conditions of Japanese occupation, when the island was renamed Syonan.

1 Architecture and Design
The museum was built to Sir Henry McCallum's design in 1887. The Neo-Palladian architecture **(above)** was joined in 2006 by a stunning Modernist structure by local W Architects that more than doubled the size of the building.

2 Singapore History Gallery
A spiral path leads to a fragment of the 14th-century Singapore Stone (see p15) and the Revere Bell **(right)**. Ceramics, jewelry, and coins recount trading before Stamford Raffles arrived.

3 Modern Colony Gallery
This gallery explores the cosmopolitan nature of the city and the lives of wealthy residents during the 1920s and 1930s **(left)**. There is a focus on the role of women in what was for them a time of progressive education and increasingly visible public life.

6 Life in Singapore: The Past 100 Years
The four interesting permanent galleries on Level 2 of the old wing comprise the Life in Singapore exhibition, including the Surviving Syonan, Modern Colony, Growing Up, and Voices of Singapore galleries.

8 Growing Up Gallery

The 1950s and 1960s were a turbulent period. Growing Up **(left)** shows how post-war children grew up amid social upheaval, and explores how villages, schools, and entertainment venues helped them to evolve a sense of self.

THE ROTUNDA DOME

The National Museum's most iconic architectural feature is the Rotunda Dome. Between 2004 and 2005, all 50 pieces of stained glass were removed from the dome and carefully restored, a lengthy and painstaking process. The final effect is stunning. On a clear day, the sun filtering through the Victorian floraland square patterns throws a ring of pretty colored lights on the floor.

Key to Floorplan
- Basement
- First Floor
- Second Floor
- Third Floor

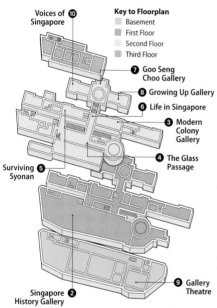

Voices of Singapore 10

7 Goo Seng Choo Gallery

8 Growing Up Gallery

6 Life in Singapore

3 Modern Colony Gallery

4 The Glass Passage

Surviving 5 Syonan

Singapore 2 History Gallery

9 Gallery Theatre

9 Gallery Theatre

The museum holds regular film screenings, theater performances, and retrospectives in its 247-seat theater.

10 Voices of Singapore

Focusing on the 1970s and 1980s, this gallery explores how locals formed a distinct national identity while maintaining their varied cultural roots **(below)**.

7 Goo Seng Choo Gallery

This holds a selection of botanical illustrations from the William Farquhar Collection of National History Drawings. Watercolor studies of regional flora are enriched by "smell stations," featuring some of the plants.

NEED TO KNOW

MAP L1 ■ 93 Stamford Rd ■ 6332-3659 ■ www. nationalmuseum.sg

Open 10am–7pm daily

Adm S$15 adults, S$10 children (free for children 6 years and below), students, and senior citizens

Last admission to the Glass Rotunda at 6.15pm; all other galleries at 6.30pm

Disabled access

■ The museum has two restaurants and a café, offering snacks or meals. Try Flutes on the first floor (see p93).

Singapore River

Flowing past the 1920s godowns (warehouses), the bars and restaurants of Clarke Quay, and the skyscrapers of the financial district, the Singapore River has always been at the center of city life. The river was the first thing to attract Sir Thomas Stamford Raffles, the city's founder, and a walk along the banks still offers some of the city's most iconic views. Better still, step aboard one of the bumboats that once jostled for space around Boat Quay. Since an intensive clean-up operation in 1987, the river has become Singapore's emotional heart. It may no longer be the main artery of commerce, but it has moved on from its polluted past.

1 Riverboat Trips

Old-fashioned bumboats take around 40 minutes to cruise along the river, past the quays and across Marina Bay. Payment is via booths by the riverside. Tourist boats provide tour commentary via a pre-recorded tape.

2 Boat Quay

The quay hasn't stopped buzzing since Chinese merchants first built their godowns here in 1820. Most of the boats have gone, and the quay is now lined with bars and restaurants.

3 Asian Civilisations Museum

Built in 1867, these riverfront former government offices were reopened as the Asian Civilisations Museum in 2003 (see p39).

4 Elgin Bridge

The oldest river crossing point was but a wooden drawbridge in 1822. The current bridge, completed in 1929, is named after the Earl of Elgin, Governor General of India in the 1960s.

NEED TO KNOW

Raffles' Landing Site: **MAP L3**; Riverboat trips can be boarded at various points along the river, including here.

Asian Civilisations Museum: **MAP M3**; 1 Empress Place; 6332-7798; open 10am–7pm daily (until 9pm Fri); adm; www.acm.org.sg

Old Parliament House: **MAP M3**; 1 Old Parliament Lane; 6332-6900; open 10am–10pm daily; events ticketed; www.theartshouse.com

G-MAX Reverse Bungy, GX-5 Xtreme Swing: www.gmaxgx5.sg/

■ A Singapore River Cruise boat trip is the best way to appreciate the skyline (see p109).

5 Clarke Quay

Singapore's favorite evening spot, Clarke Quay is the river's largest conservation project **(below)**. Godowns have been renovated to create a fashionable hub of waterfront bars and restaurants.

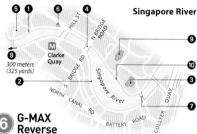

Singapore River

6 G-MAX Reverse Bungy, GX-5 Xtreme Swing

Thrill-seekers can fling themselves skywards for an alternative view of the Colonial District. Both rides are only recommended for those with a strong stomach.

7 Cavenagh Bridge

Designed as a draw-bridge and built in Glasgow, this bridge was named after a former governor. Long since pedestrianized, it has a Victorian sign forbidding the passage of livestock.

THE SINGAPORE STONE

On display in the National Museum *(see pp12–13)*, this fragment of inscribed sandstone remains a mystery. Part of a rock discovered at the mouth of the river in 1819, its 50 lines of inscription eluded translation by scholars including Raffles. The rock was blown up in 1843 on the orders of a British engineer. This piece is one of at least three surviving relics.

8 Robertson Quay

As trade thrived, the swampland upriver was reclaimed and used to build godowns, creating Robertson Quay. The redeveloped area is now a popular metropolitan waterfront scene, lined with chic restaurants, bars, and galleries.

9 Old Parliament House

Singapore's oldest building **(below)**, erected in 1827, was named Parliament House after Singapore gained its independence in 1965 *(see p42)*.

10 Raffles' Landing Site

The spot at which Raffles landed is marked by a marble statue **(above)**, a cast of the original at the Victoria Theatre and Concert Hall. It is framed to the north by the Colonial District and to the south by the Central Business District towers.

Thian Hock Keng Temple

Built in 1839, this is one of Singapore's oldest Chinese temples. It was raised by sailors in homage to the goddess Ma Zu, who, it is believed, laid down her life to give seafarers a safe passage. The temple, paid for by individual donors such as Hokkien leader Tan Tock Seng, was constructed without the use of nails in the southern Chinese architectural style. It is laid out along a traditional north-south axis, with shrines to several deities.

1 Door Paintings

Paintings on the door depict auspicious creatures (left). In Taoist tradition, these protect the temple. A plank across the threshold keeps ghosts away, and ensures visitors bow heads upon entering.

2 Construction

Craftsmen from Southern China built the temple in the traditional manner using no nails. All of the building materials were imported from China, including ironwood for the pillars and pottery used in the roof's mosaics.

3 The Front Step

The temple was originally located on the banks of the river, but extensive land reclamation has since cut it off from the water's edge. The raised step protected it from the high tides that once lapped at its foundations.

4 The Ceiling

During the renovation of the temple in 2000, artists from China were brought in to restore the carvings on the ceiling under the main altar, and to return the gold leaf and bright paintwork to their original splendor.

5 Guan Yin, the Goddess of Mercy

In the courtyard behind the main altar sits Guan Yin (below), the Goddess of Mercy. She is said to have rejected nirvana to return to earth especially to help the needy and those less fortunate.

NEED TO KNOW

MAP L4 ■ 158 Telok Ayer St ■ 6423-4616 ■ www.thianhockkeng. com.sg

Open 7:30am–5:30pm daily

■ Thian Hock Keng celebrates festivals such as the Chinese Lunar New Year and the birthdays of Guan Yin and Ma Zu with prayer, traditional music, and dance. Since all Chinese holidays are guided by the lunar calendar, it is best to ask the temple exactly when these holidays fall.

■ At the corner of Telok Ayer and Amoy streets, a popular hawker center offers drinks, local dishes, and fruit.

8 Ancestral Tablets

In keeping with the Taoist practice of ancestor worship, ancestral tablets **(left)** inscribed with the names and dates of departed devotees, are regularly tended with offerings of incense, food, and prayers.

ETIQUETTE IN CHINESE TEMPLES

As in any place of worship, respect for devotees deep in prayer is appreciated. Taking photos is permitted, but visitors must refrain from touching anything on altars. Unlike in Hindu temples or Muslim mosques, clothing norms here are relaxed. Shorts and sleeveless tops are allowed, and footwear can be worn inside the temple.

Thian Hock Keng Temple

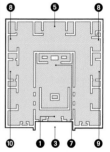

6 Chong Hock Girls' School

Next door to the temple is one of Singapore's first girls' schools **(above)**, funded by the Huay Kuan, a Hokkien community association. Such clan associations were the backbone of the local Chinese.

7 Ma Zu, the Guardian of the South Seas

The main hall contains an image of Ma Zu, the sea goddess and a patron of seafarers. She was born in AD 960 in China's southern Fujian province, and risked her life to save fishermen and sailors.

9 Statue of Confucius

Confucius **(below)**, one of China's greatest thinkers (551-497 BC), developed a social value system that promoted self-discipline, respect for family, education, and political responsibility – values that continue to shape Chinese society today.

10 Statue of Chen Zhi Guang

This 8th-century Chinese governor was so successful in developing the economy and improving living standards for the poor that the Hokkien people came to worship him as a deity.

TOP10 ⭐ Sultan Mosque

The Sultan Mosque is located in the neighborhood that, in 1819, was assigned to the Malay Sultan of Johor who ruled Singapore. The original mosque that stood on this site was constructed in 1824. Partially funded by the East India Company, it was the style of mosque typically found in Southeast Asia, with a low, two-tiered roof like a pyramid. A century later, the old mosque had fallen into a state of disrepair and was replaced. Swan & Maclaren, the local architects responsible for many landmark buildings, designed it.

4 The Bottle Band

Around the base of the main onion dome is an unusual architectural feature. This is a wide black band made from rows of bottles stacked on their sides, five or six bottles high. Their bottoms appear to glisten like black and brown jewels in the sun.

1 The Central Prayer Hall

Large enough to fit 5,000 devotees, the main hall (above) is for men only, while women occupy the galleries above. The carpet, donated by a Saudi Arabian prince, bears his emblem.

2 The Mihrab

The *mihrab* is a small niche that marks the direction of Mecca, and it is from where the imam leads the congregation in prayer five times a day. This altar is decorated with intricately patterned gold motifs.

3 The Mimbar

On Fridays, the Muslim holy day, the imam delivers his sermon, or *khutba*, to a full prayer hall. He does so from the *mimbar*, an elaborate pulpit atop a staircase reserved for the purpose (right).

NEED TO KNOW

MAP H5 ■ 3 Muscat St ■ 6293-4405

Open 10am–noon & 2–4pm daily (2:30–4pm on Fri)

■ After sunset during Ramadan, the month of fasting, the streets around the mosque fill with stalls and stores selling delicious Malay treats.

■ Sip Turkish or Malay-style tea or fresh lime juice in the cafés along Bussorah Street, opposite the mosque.

Sultan Mosque

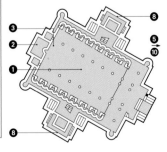

MOSQUE ETIQUETTE

Non-Muslims are welcome to visit the mosque, but they are advised not to enter the main prayer hall. Viewing is allowed from the surrounding courtyard and corridors, however. Appropriate dress, such as pants or long skirts and shirts with sleeves, is required. The mosque provides robes at the entrance for visitors dressed inappropriately. Footwear must be taken off outside.

9 Architectural Design

The mosque is built in Saracenic style **(left)**, combining Persian, Moorish, and Turkish design including pointed arches, minarets, and domes. The interior is adorned with calligraphic verses and mosaics.

10 The Annex

Mosques serve many purposes for Muslims – providing space for education, religious rituals, and community development programs. The annex at the Sultan Mosque, built in 1993, offers these services to the local Muslim community.

5 The Maqam

At the rear of the mosque is a *maqam*, or mausoleum, containing the graves of several members of the Royal Family, including the grandson of Sultan Hussein, who signed over Singapore to Sir Stamford Raffles in 1819.

6 Mosque Alignment

Most mosques are built with the prayer hall facing the holy city of Mecca. For this reason, North Bridge Road has a distinct bend to allow for the correct alignment of Sultan Mosque.

7 The Domes

A tradition in mosque architecture, the onion dome originates from Turkey and the Middle East. It creates a roofline distinguishable above the city's low-rise buildings. At the top of each of the gold domes stands the star and crescent – a traditional symbol of Islam.

8 Ablutions

Two areas have faucets, for worshipers to wash their hands, faces, and feet before prayers. Ablutions, or *wudhu* **(right)**, purify the body and soul.

TOP 10 ★ Sri Veeramakaliamman Temple

In the mid-19th century, Indian laborers who settled in what is now Little India built a Hindu shrine there. The original temple, a small nondescript structure, was demolished in 1983 to make way for the one that stands here today. It took three years to build, at great cost, with artisans brought from India. The temple is dedicated to the goddess Kali, which is why Hindus who worship here leave with red ash smeared on their foreheads; those who pray at temples for male deities receive white ash. This is one of Singapore's oldest holy sites.

1 Kali
Occupying central position on the main altar, Kali **(above)** is the Divine Mother and Destroyer of Evil. She represents the cycle of birth through death – her name is Sanskrit for "endless time."

2 Muruga
This is the name given to the God of War – the six-headed deity who grants great success to his devotees. Muruga is worshipped mainly by Tamils, the majority of the city's Indians.

3 The Altar of the Nine Planets
Each single planet is represented on this altar at which devotees pray to their zodiac sign. Jewelry stores nearby sell rings adorned with nine stones, placed according to the astrological alignment of the wearer.

4 Ganesh
Distinguishable by his elephant's head, Ganesh **(right)** is the most worshipped of all Hindu deities. As the Remover of Obstacles, he is invoked at the start of prayers to help clear the mind, and consulted at the start of any new ventures.

5 Washing of the Deities
On the right side of the main altar, a small spout drains the water that rinsed the deities during their morning cleansing ritual. This holy water is used in prayer.

6 The Gopuram

Rows of figures, which are representations of deities, top the main gate *(gopuram)* and the roof. On holy days, when the temple is full, devotees can appreciate them from outside.

7 Smashing Coconuts

Before entering the temple, devotees smash coconuts in a small metal box. This is symbolic of shattering their obstacles to spiritual concentration. These coconuts even have "eyes" carved into them, which are meant to "see" the obstacles in a devotee's path and destroy them.

ETIQUETTE IN HINDU TEMPLES

Visitors must remove footwear before they enter, and also wear appropriate attire – legs must be covered, and shirts should at least have short sleeves. In Indian culture, the left hand is reserved for toilet tasks, so pointing toward a person or sacred object with the left hand is impolite. If you must point, use your open hand. You should also turn off cell phones before entering.

9 Sri Lakshmi Durgai

While many Hindu figures and deities appear aggressive, Sri Lakshmi Durgai is represented as beautiful and graceful. According to Hindu belief, the goddess with three eyes and 18 arms will bring peace and joy to those devotees who pray to her.

NEED TO KNOW

MAP F3 ■ 141 Serangoon Rd ■ 6295-4538 ■ www.sriveeramakaliamman.com

Open 8am–12:30pm & 4–8:30pm daily

■ During Deepavali *(see p67)*, the most significant holiday for local Hindus, the temple is illuminated with tiny candles, symbols of the eternal light of the soul.

■ The coffee shop opposite, at the corner of Serangoon and Norris roads, serves *chapatis* (Indian bread) as well as good, cheap curries.

8 Sri Periachi

In one corner of the compound, a dais holds the statue of the fierce Sri Periachi. Despite being depicted amid blood and gore, she is the goddess of fertility, childbirth, and the good health of newborns.

10 Roof Figures

On the main temple's roof are carved figures that tell stories from Hindu lore **(below)**, such as how Ganesh ended up with his elephant's head.

Following pages Detail of the gate to the Thian Hock Keng Temple

🔟 ⭐ Singapore Botanic Gardens

This park is one of the finest botanical gardens in Southeast Asia and Singapore's sole UNESCO World Heritage Site. The park was founded in 1859 as a pleasure garden, and pathways meander through a tropical landscape that showcases the region's natural habitats and species. There are avenues of frangipanis and scarlet lipstick palms, and wide, sloping lawns adorned with trees and sculptures. On weekends, the park is packed with families, joggers, and dog walkers, but in the week, it is an oasis of calm.

National Orchid Garden ①

This beautiful enclosure opened in 1995 **(right)**. It contains over 1,000 orchid species and 2,000 hybrids. Some hybrids are named in honor of visiting heads of state as well as international dignitaries. It is the only garden with an admission fee *(see p47)*.

② Vanda Miss Joaquim

There is debate over whether this hybrid of pink, violet, and orange-rose was discovered or bred by Miss Agnes Joaquim in 1893. It is a lovely orchid **(right)**, and was chosen as Singapore's national flower in 1981.

④ Healing Garden

This garden features over 400 species of plants with healing properties. It is designed in the shape of a human body, and plants are then arranged thematically, in relation to where their efficacy lies.

③ The Lakes

The gardens have three lakes. Swan Lake is named for its white swans, while ducks and black swans enjoy Eco Lake. Outdoor concerts are held on a stage in the middle of Symphony Lake **(left)**.

5 Sculptures

Several sculptures in the gardens celebrate the families who come to play on weekends. Favorites include *Joy* (left), overlooking Swan Lake, *The Girl on a Bicycle* who freewheels along the top of a spiral hedge, and *Girl on a Swing* who pauses mid-air.

6 Palm Valley

Developed in 1879, after the colonial government took over the gardens' management, Palm Valley is home to more than 220 species of native and non-native palms. Among them are the large talipot palm and the traveler's palm, with its distinctive fan shape.

7 Children's Garden

At the Jacob Ballas Children's Garden, children under 12 are encouraged to discover life sciences through play, and to investigate the role of plants and water in everyday life. Visitors should carry sunscreen and a change of clothing.

8 Bandstand

This octagonal structure was erected in the 1930s as a stage for performances by military bands. Although it no longer serves this purpose, it remains a central feature of the gardens.

"MAD" RIDLEY

Henry Ridley, a young British botanist, became the first director of the Botanic Gardens in 1888 and spent the next 23 years developing their horticultural potential. In the late 19th century, he devised a way to tap rubber without damaging the trees. Convinced of the crop's potential, he lobbied planters so zealously that he became known as "Mad Ridley."

9 Rain Forest

The park's first designers recognized the importance of the indigenous forest and preserved an area of rain forest, where ancient trees (above) continue to thrive today.

10 The Ginger Garden

Several hundred kinds of ginger are displayed in this interesting garden, along with other ornamental and edible species (left), including lilies and turmeric. The waterfall provides a great photo opportunity.

NEED TO KNOW

MAP S2 ▪ 1 Cluny Rd ▪ 6471-7361 ▪ www.sbg.org.sg

Open 5am–midnight daily

National Orchid Garden: open 8am–7pm; adults S$5, senior citizens S$1, children free

▪ Free outdoor concerts take place at the Shaw Foundation Symphony Stage at weekends. Check www.sbg.org.sg or contact the visitor service centers.

TOP 10 ⭐ Singapore Zoo, Night Safari, and River Safari

The Singapore Zoo, and its Night Safari and River Safari offshoots, are three neighboring sights offering the chance to see thousands of animals living in conditions that resemble their natural habitats. The Night Safari is especially popular, allowing visitors to view nocturnal creatures when they are most active. Part zoo, part aquarium, the River Safari showcases the wildlife of some of the world's great rivers, including the Nile, Mississippi, and Yangtze. Interactive exhibits, shows, and programs, all in English, educate visitors about the animals and their behavior.

3 Free-Ranging Orangutan Exhibit

With platforms, trees, and vines, this zoo exhibit **(right)** re-creates the orangutans' natural habitat, permitting the animals to climb, swing, and play as they would in the wild.

1 Night Safari

Muted lighting allows visitors to observe animals such as clouded leopards, wallabies, and barking deer, after dark. It also stages shows, such as the Thumbuakar performance **(above)**.

4 Amazon River Quest

This waterborne ride at the River Safari takes you past enclosures of Amazonian wildlife, including Brazilian tapirs and scarlet ibises.

5 Giant Panda Forest

Living under an air-conditioned dome, giant pandas Kai Kai and Jia Jia are the River Safari's star couple. Also housed here is the raccoon-like red panda.

2 Great Rift Valley of Ethiopia

The highlight of this award-winning zoo exhibit is its troop of almost 80 baboons **(below)**. There are also Nubian ibexes, black-backed jackals, storks, and banded mongooses.

6 Jungle Breakfast

Visitors are invited to join playful orangutans and other friendly residents for breakfast, one of the most popular activities at the zoo. This is also the best time to visit the zoo, while the air is still cool and the zoo is quiet.

7 Fragile Forest

Housed in a giant biodome in the zoo, this area replicates a rain forest environment for ring-tailed lemurs **(left)**, sloths, flying foxes, and other animals. Visitors can observe them as they go about their activities.

ZOO GUIDE

The Singapore Zoo, Night Safari, and River Safari are three separate parks located side by side. All are operated by Wildlife Reserves Singapore. While the zoo is best toured on foot, there is also a tram, which costs extra. Visitors can also take a tram at the Night Safari, although this is not included in the park entry fee either. It operates an enjoyable circular route, with a number of stops at which visitors can alight and explore the trails.

8 Feeding Times

Keepers will be on hand to provide a fun and informative commentary while the animals are at their most active – during feeding time. In selected exhibits, such as for the giraffes and elephants, early visitors may have the opportunity to help feed the animals themselves.

9 Animal Friends

The Zoo is also home to domestic animals, many of whom were once abandoned pets. In the "Animal Friends" show, mice, cats, and dogs display their special abilities, highlighting the bonds they have with their dedicated trainers.

10 Wild Africa

Landscaped to resemble the African savannah, this zoo area is home to grass-grazing mammals and their predators **(below)**. There are platforms for looking giraffes in the eye and a cheetah observation hut.

NEED TO KNOW

MAP S1 ■ 80 Mandai Lake Rd ■ 6269-3411

Zoo: open 8:30am– 6pm daily; adm S$33 adults, S$22 children; www.zoo.com.sg

Night Safari: open 7:15pm–midnight daily; adm S$45 adults, S$30 children; www.nightsafari.com.sg

River Safari: open 10am–7pm daily; adm S$30 adults, S$20 children; www.riversafari.com.sg

See websites for online discounts, and details of combination tickets covering two or all three attractions.

■ It can take an hour to reach the zoo by public transportation from the city center. Private bus companies operate from various hotels and attractions downtown to the zoo (Singapore Attractions Express www.saex.com.sg).

■ Experiences such as the "Jungle Breakfast" cost extra, as do some rides.

TOP 10 ⭐ Marina Bay

Built on reclaimed land, creating a freshwater reservoir in the process, the Marina Bay area offers great views of the cityscape. Besides extending Singapore's banking district, Marina Bay includes green spaces, notably Gardens by the Bay, as well as shopping malls and luxury residential high-rises. Most eye-catching is the giant boat-shape structure on top of Marina Bay Sands resort, designed by Moshe Safdie, but surreal architectural marvels abound. Walking around the entirety of the Bay is possible along a 2-mile (3.5-km) waterfront promenade, crossing pedestrian bridges.

Gardens by the Bay and the impressive structure of Marina Bay Sands Resort

1 Gardens by the Bay

One of Singapore's top attractions, these extraordinary gardens contain over 1 million plants. The green towers of the Supertree Grove, two vast biodomes, free events, and excellent eating options keep visitors busy (see p46).

2 Esplanade – Theatres on the Bay

The spiked aluminium double-domes of Esplanade host world-class concerts, theater, dance, and visual arts events (see p42). It also contains a library, an art gallery, shops and dining, including Makansutra hawker center (see p61).

3 Marina Bay Sands

This integrated resort incorporates a five-star hotel (left), restaurants and nightlife, a casino, theaters, the ArtScience Museum, and The Shoppes luxury mall. On the 57th floor, there's an observation deck, an infinity pool, and a bar.

4 ArtScience Museum

Shaped like a lotus flower (above), this museum on the water's edge fuses design, science, and technology in its displays. As well as the permanent ArtScience Gallery, ten extended "fingers" host travelling science exhibitions that are usually family-friendly.

5 Marina Barrage

This concrete dam can be crossed 24/7. The Sustainable Singapore Gallery – located on the western side of the dam – is free, with a huge grassy rooftop above that is popular with kite-flyers and picnickers.

6 The Skyline

Singapore's tallest skyscrapers, One Raffles Place, UOB Plaza One, and Republic Plaza, rise above Shenton Way, the city's downtown financial district, while the water's edge is flanked by low-rise heritage buildings.

8 Helix Bridge

Linking Marina South to Marina Centre, this curved-steel pedestrian bridge was inspired by the structure of DNA. It offers superb views of the Bay, particularly the ArtScience Museum, from its viewing platforms, and it is lit at night.

SINGAPORE FLYER EXPERIENCES

For an unforgettable Flyer experience, there are three luxury options. The first two – the Singapore Sling Flight and the Premium Champagne Flight – are accompanied by a drink. The Premium Sky Dining Flight offers a four-course Western, Chinese, or vegetarian meal, plus two rotations on the wheel.

9 Singapore Flyer

The largest observation wheel in Asia looms an impressive 541 ft (165 m) above Marina Bay. It offers expansive views over the Singapore River, from the Colonial District out to the neighboring islands in the distance.

7 Clifford Pier

Built in 1933, this Art Deco pier was the main landing point for sea travelers and, postwar, a departure point for ferries to southern islands. Its soaring arches now form an airy restaurant serving top-notch local cuisine and afternoon tea.

10 The Merlion

Half-fish and half-lion, the Merlion symbolizes the unity of the lion city and the sea. Guarding the Singapore River like an ancient mythical beast, the current statue was unveiled in 1972.

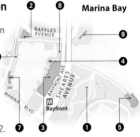

Marina Bay

NEED TO KNOW

Singapore Flyer: **MAP P3**; 30 Raffles Avenue; 6333-3311; open 8:30am–10pm daily; adm: adult S$33, children (3–12 years old) S$21; www.singaporeflyer.com

Gardens by the Bay: **MAP P4**; 18 Marina Gardens Drive; 6420-6848; open 5am–2am daily; Conservatories 9am–9pm

daily; adm S$28 adults, S$15 children; www.gardensbythebay.com.sg

ArtScience Museum: **MAP N3**; 6 Bayfront Avenue; 6688-8626; open 10am–7pm daily; adm; www.marinabaysands.com

Sustainable Singapore Gallery: **MAP T3**; Marina Barrage, 8 Marina Gardens Drive; 6514-5959; open

9am–9pm Wed–Mon; www.pub.gov.sg/marinabarrage

▪ The casino at Marina Bay Sands is free for foreigners. The dress code is smart casual – no beach wear, shorts, or flip flops.

▪ The two theaters at MBS provide great family entertainment, with musicals and touring Broadway shows.

🔟 ⭐ Raffles Hotel

Behind the famous facade of Singapore's grandest old lady is a labyrinth of tropical courtyards and verandas. Raffles Hotel was founded by the Armenian Sarkies brothers in a beachfront bungalow in 1887. It was saved from demolition when it was declared a National Monument during its centennial – and multimillion-dollar renovations ensure the hotel maintains its colonial grandeur. With a range of restaurants, boutiques, galleries, bars, and a museum, Raffles is a destination in its own right.

① The Long Bar
Birthplace of the Singapore Sling, this must be the only bar in the city where guests are encouraged to litter peanut shells.

② Architectural Restoration
The Raffles Hotel known today was unveiled in 1991 after three years of restoration work costing S$160 million. A little over 25 years later, further work ensures the hotel maintains its position as the grande dame of Singapore's luxury hotels.

③ The Hotel
Character and opulence come at a price, but few hotels can match Raffles' blend of history, luxury, and colonial ambience. The hotel's famous and exotically dressed Sikh doormen are charming and patient with photo requests (**left**).

Raffles Hotel exterior

④ Writers Bar
A quieter place to sip a Sling, this elegant bar is located in the hotel's colonial lobby. Browse the works of former guests Somerset Maugham, Joseph Conrad, and Rudyard Kipling. The resident pianist plays a range of musical genres.

⑤ Afternoon Tea at the Tiffin Room
The most refined of all traditions at Raffles Hotel has to be the afternoon tea. Finger sandwiches, pastries, and scones with clotted cream accompany a choice of Pascal Hamour teas, with dim sum for Asian palates.

⑥ Gift Shop
The Raffles palm motif adorns everything, from slippers to hats, in the hotel's extensive gift shop. Fancy bottles of pre-mixed spirits for creating Singapore Slings at home make a compact memento.

8 The Raffles 1915 Gin

Marking the centenary of the Singapore Sling, this gin was created in association with London-based microdistillery Sipsmith, whose co-founder was Stamford Raffles' progeny.

10 Raffles Grill

All of Raffles' restaurants maintain high standards, none more so than the swankiest of the lot, Raffles Grill **(below)**.

7 Bar and Billiard Room

Legend has it that Singapore's last tiger was shot under the billiards table in 1902. Guests can play a round of billiards **(below)** or enjoy a quiet drink here.

9 Raffles Courtyard

This open-air restaurant, amid palm trees and serving Italian cuisine, is an excellent spot to enjoy the hotel's refined and tranquil ambience.

NEED TO KNOW

MAP M1 ■ 1 Beach Rd ■ 6337-1886 ■ www.raffles.com

■ A three-phase restoration means that the hotel is closed to guests and visitors until its grand reopening, scheduled for mid-2018. Check the website for details of the restoration work and future opening timings.

🔟 ⭐ Sentosa

Sentosa is Singapore's pleasure island – a local getaway dedicated to recreation. There is something for everyone here; attractions include award-winning spa retreats, golf courses, and a marina. Pleasant man-made beaches lie alongside lush wooded slopes, with plenty of bars and restaurants nearby. The island was originally called Pulau Blakang Mati, meaning "death from behind," possibly because of the pirates that once attacked its shores. It was later renamed Sentosa, which means "peace and tranquillity."

1 S.E.A. Aquarium

Amid some stunningly vast tanks **(below)**, the show-stopper is the Open Ocean zone, home to sharks and manta rays. Also here is the Maritime Experiential Museum *(see p39)*.

2 Images of Singapore LIVE!

This museum retells Singapore's fascinating history using costumed actors and a mini boat ride. The ride ends at Madame Tussauds wax museum.

3 Sentosa Golf Club

The two courses here are challenging and have great harbour views. The Tanjong course features natural lakes and an undulating fairway. The Serapong course is home to the Singapore Open.

NEED TO KNOW

MAP S3 ■ Sentosa Island ■ 1800-736-8672 ■ www.sentosa.com.sg

Open 24 hours daily

Adm S$1; if driving to Sentosa, you must pay a flat fee that varies according to the time of visit

⋯⋯⋯⋯⋯⋯⋯⋯⋯⋯⋯⋯⋯

■ **Tanjong Beach has the best sunset views on the island.**

■ **Coastes, overlooking Siloso Beach, offers multiple dining options, serving drinks and international food all day long.**

Sentosa Island

TRAVEL TIPS

The simplest way to reach Sentosa is to walk from VivoCity mall via the Sentosa Gateway bridge. Alternatively, ride the Sentosa monorail from Sentosa Station (VivoCity) to Beach Station. Free Bus 1, Bus 2, and Bus 3 ply around Sentosa 7am–11pm Sun–Thu, and 7am–12:30am Fri–Sat. Car and taxi passengers entering Sentosa must pay the entrance fee at booths near Sentosa Island.

6 Siloso Beach
This beach **(left)** is where the young and beautiful hang out, sunbathing and playing volleyball. Several beach bars and stores operate during the day, although the pace (and volume) picks up at sunset.

7 So SPA by Sofitel
The largest So SPA outlet in the world, this spa at the Sofitel has 14 indoor treatment rooms, six outdoor pavilions, and a variety of facilities for guests to choose from.

9 Singapore Cable Car
The glass cabins of the cable car offer a pricey but exciting way to arrive at Sentosa from Mount Faber (see p100) via Harbour Front. From its Imbiah Lookout terminus, a branch line **(below)** takes you to the western tip of the island.

4 Sentosa 4D AdventureLand
Billed as Southeast Asia's first 4D theater, AdventureLand features a state-of-the-art digital projection system, surround-sound, and seats that move with the on-screen action. The effects include mist spray in water scenes.

5 Fort Siloso
Original features at this fort recreate the life of colonial soldiers. Special effects include battle sounds and recreations of Japan's surrender (see p44).

8 Skyline Luge Sentosa
A cross between a toboggan and a go-cart, the luge is great fun for all ages. Take the Skyride chairlift to the top of the hill and meander your way back down again as fast as you dare. Each cart has sophisticated speed controls for safety and the young can ride tandem with an adult **(left)**.

10 Sentosa Nature Discovery
Long-tailed macaque monkeys, wild white cockatoos, and insect-eating pitcher plants can be seen on this walk through Sentosa's forest. Though not comparable to Bukit Timah (see p102), it is still worth it.

The Top 10
of Everything

Bridges spanning the atrium of
the National Gallery Singapore

🔟 Moments in History

1 1390: Iskandar Shah
A deposed prince called Iskandar Shah declared himself ruler of the island of Temasek. Legend has it he saw a lion-like creature and renamed the island Singapura, or lion island. The Keramat at Fort Canning is said to be his tomb *(see p47)*.

2 1819: Arrival of Sir Stamford Raffles
On a mission to find new sites for the East India Company, Stamford Raffles stepped ashore at Singapore. Convinced it could be a strategic trading site, he persuaded a Malay noble to sign a treaty giving exclusive rights to Britain.

3 1824: British East India Company
The East India Company secured legal rule of the island. Tariff-free trade was enticing, and the village quickly became a town. In 1826, Singapore was declared capital of the Straits Settlements and became a flourishing Crown Colony by 1867.

4 1869: Suez Canal
The opening of the Suez Canal in Egypt transformed Singapore's trading potential by opening new markets and reducing travel distance between Europe and Asia.

Trade on the Suez Canal

Goods arriving by steam ship

5 1873: Steam Ship Travel
The development of coal-powered steam ships brought more reliable shipping schedules. Singapore quickly became a major refuelling port, employing thousands of porters to heave coal.

6 1907: Rubber and Tin
New technologies demanded new materials. Rubber seedlings grown in the Botanic Gardens *(see pp24–5)* were used to create Singapore's first rubber plantation. Meanwhile, the first smelter for producing tin opened at Pulau Brani to satisfy the demands of America's new canning industry.

7 1942: World War II
After a Japanese attack sank HMS *Repulse* and the *Prince of Wales*, British forces retreated down the Malay peninsula, blowing up the causeway to delay the invasion.

Singapore fell on February 15, 1942, and an estimated 50,000 people, mainly Chinese Singaporeans, died during the three-year Japanese occupation of the island.

8 1959: Singapore's Self-Government

After many years of negotiation, the British agreed to hold general elections, resulting in a landslide victory for the People's Action Party, which promised a Singapore united with Malaya and fully independent of Britain.

First prime minister, Lee Kuan Yew

9 1959: Lee Kuan Yew

Lee Kuan Yew became the island's first prime minister on June 3, 1959. Revered by Singaporeans as the father of the nation, Lee remained a towering figure in Asian politics until his death in 2015.

10 1965: Singapore's Independence

Singapore became part of the Federation of Malaysia in 1963. However, political and racial tensions led to riots in 1964, and, on August 9, 1965, Lee announced a separation from Malaysia and the Republic of Singapore was born.

TOP 10 SINGAPORE READS

Film adaptation of *Lord Jim*

1 *King Rat* by James Clavell
Drawing on Clavell's experience as a Changi POW in World War II, his novel weighs the costs of survival.

2 *Lord Jim* by Joseph Conrad
When the crew of a stricken ship abandons its passengers, one officer is left to answer for his actions.

3 *Saint Jack* by Paul Theroux
A tale of an ageing, seedy expatriate who tries to start a brothel in the city.

4 *The Singapore Grip* by J. G. Farrell
A satirical novel about a privileged expatriate family on the eve of the Japanese invasion.

5 *Snake Wine: A Singapore Episode* by Patrick Anderson
English-born Canadian poet Anderson presents a picture of a 1950s Singapore that is now almost unrecognizable.

6 *First Loves* by Philip Jeyaretnam
Tales of life in Singapore's cultural melting pot in a series of short stories.

7 *Little Ironies: Stories of Singapore* by Catherine Lim
Short stories that look at Singaporean life and society in the 1970s.

8 *The Singapore Story: Memoirs of Lee Kuan Yew*
Singapore's first PM lists the events that shaped a nation.

9 *A History of Singapore* by C. M. Turnbull
Tracing Singapore's history from Raffles' arrival to 1988.

10 *Rogue Trader* by Nick Leeson
An account of how Barings Bank trader Leeson lost a billion dollars, and spent four years in Changi prison.

🔟 Museums

1 National Gallery Singapore

1 St. Andrew's Rd ▪ 6271-7000 ▪ Open 10am–7pm daily (10am–10pm Fri & Sat) ▪ Adm ▪ www.nationalgallery.sg

Opened in 2015, this gallery houses a fine collection of local and East Asian artwork, and plays host to top traveling exhibitions.

National Gallery Singapore

2 Peranakan Museum

MAP L1 ▪ 39 Armenian St ▪ 6332-7591 ▪ Open 10am–7pm daily (10am–9pm Fri) ▪ Adm (half-price 7–9pm Fri) ▪ www.peranakanmuseum.org.sg

This museum explores the culture of the Peranakans, people born of intermarriage between local women and foreign traders from countries such as China and India. The mix of two distinct communities is seen in a range of spectacular works of art – jewelry, furniture, beadwork, porcelain, and other treasures.

3 Lee Kong Chian Natural History Museum

2 Conservatory Drive, National University of Singapore ▪ 6601-3333 ▪ Open 10am–7pm Tue–Sun ▪ Adm: adults S$21, students and senior citizens S$13 ▪ www.lkcnhm.nus.edu.sg

One of Singapore's best-kept secrets, this museum houses a splendid collection of biological specimens illustrating the marvelous diversity of nature. There's also useful background on Singapore's flora, fauna, and geology.

4 Malay Heritage Centre

MAP H4 ▪ 85 Sultan Gate ▪ 6391-0450 ▪ Open 10am–6pm Tue–Sun (last adm 5:30pm) ▪ Adm ▪ www.malayheritage.org.sg

Formely a palace used by royals of the Johor sultanate, the Malay Heritage Centre was redeveloped in 2005. It features permanent galleries, covering the history of the neighborhood, Kampong Glam. They also elucidate the culture and contribution of the Malay community.

5 Changi Museum

MAP U2 ▪ 1000 Upper Changi Rd ▪ 6214-2451 ▪ Open 9:30am–5pm daily ▪ www.changimuseum.com

This museum commemorates the World War II prisoner-of-war camp for Allied troops and civilians that was housed at Changi Prison.

6 Chinatown Heritage Centre

MAP K4 ▪ 48 Pagoda St ▪ 6221-9556 ▪ Open 9am–8pm daily (last adm 7pm) ▪ Adm: adults S$15, children (3–12 years old) S$11 ▪ www.chinatownheritagecentre.com.sg

Dioramas re-create the conditions in which early Chinese immigrants lived. Families were packed into cubicles, and battled poverty, disease, and opium addiction.

Chinatown Heritage Centre

Exhibits in the National Museum of Singapore

7 Maritime Experiential Museum

MAP S3 ■ 8 Sentosa Gateway ■ 6577-8888 ■ Open 10am–7pm daily (check website) ■ Adm ■ www.rwsentosa.com

The museum explores Asia's maritime trade, and displays some interactive exhibits. Its centerpiece is a recreation of an Arab dhow, the *Jewel of Muscat*, donated by the government of Oman.

8 Red Dot Design Museum

11 Marina Boulevard ■ www.museum.red-dot.sg

Asia's largest design museum accommodates over 1,000 contemporary design and communication products. The artifacts on display are all winners of the Red Dot Design Award, one of the world's most renowned design competitions.

9 Asian Civilisations Museum

Housed in Empress Place Building on the riverfront, this museum explores the history, art, and culture of Asia, with 1,300 artifacts that include Islamic art, Indonesian shrines, and textiles *(see pp14–15)*.

Asian Civilisations Museum artifact

10 National Museum of Singapore

Dating back to 1849, Singapore's oldest museum is also its best, telling the island's whirlwind story from the 14th century to the present. The various exhibits are interesting to visitors of all ages, and history buffs can enjoy eyewitness accounts on the free audio companion *(see pp12–13)*.

TOP 10 Places of Worship

1 St. Andrew's Cathedral

Named for the patron saint of Scotland, this Anglican church is on a piece of land selected by Raffles himself. Inside the church is the Canterbury Stone, presented by the Metropolitan Cathedral Church of Canterbury. The Coventry Cross is made of silver-plated nails from the ruins of Coventry Cathedral, and the Coronation Carpet is part of the one used for Queen Elizabeth II in Westminster Abbey (see p43).

2 Armenian Church

MAP L2 ■ 60 Hill St ■ 6334-0141 ■ Open 9am–6pm daily ■ www. armeniansinasia.org

Built in 1835 and dedicated to St. Gregory the Illuminator, this church was the focal point for an Armenian community that has now dwindled to almost nil. Behind the church are gravestones of prominent community members, such as the Sarkies brothers who founded the Raffles Hotel and the lady for whom the national flower, the Vanda Miss Joaquim, is named.

3 CHIJMES (Convent of the Holy Infant Jesus)

The Gothic-style chapel within this complex is Singapore's most ornate church. Although services stopped in 1983, when it became an entertainment complex, the chapel still hosts weddings and receptions. A door in the northeast corner of the grounds is the spot where abandoned babies were left to be cared for by the nuns (see p43).

4 Sri Thendayutha-pani Temple

MAP K1 ■ 15 Tank Rd ■ 6737-9393 ■ Open 8am–noon & 5:30–8:30pm daily ■ www.sttemple.com

This Hindu temple had humble beginnings as a statue of Lord Muruga under a bodhi tree. A permanent temple was built in 1859 but it was replaced by a new one in 1983. It is renovated every 12 years, in keeping with Hindu tradition.

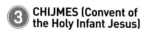

Sri Thendayuthapani Temple statue

5 Kong Meng San Phor Kork See Temple

MAP T2 ■ 88 Bright Hill Drive ■ 6849-5300 ■ Open 8am–4pm daily ■ www.kmspks.org

The largest Buddhist temple in Singapore, this 1920 complex was built to house the growing numbers of monks residing in the city. It continues to be an important monastery. The Hall of Great

CHIJMES (Convent of the Holy Infant Jesus)

Strength closes at 4pm and the Hall of Great Compassion at 4:45pm, but the compound is open till late.

6 Cathedral of the Good Shepherd

MAP M1 ■ 4 Queen St ■ 6337-2036 ■ Open 8am–9pm Mon–Fri, 7am–9pm Sat & Sun ■ www.cathedral.catholic.sg

Catholicism arrived with the Portuguese in the 1500s. Singapore's early days saw Catholic services being held in a thatched structure at Bras Basah Road. By the mid-1800s, this church had been built, along with a school, St. Joseph's Institution, and the Convent of the Holy Infant Jesus, all within close proximity. Non-Catholics are welcome for mass.

7 Maghain Aboth Synagogue

MAP L1 ■ 24 Waterloo St ■ 6337-2189 ■ Adm by prior arrangement ■ www.singaporejews.com

Jews first arrived in Singapore from Iran and Iraq in 1831. Their oldest synagogue in Singapore, Maghain Aboth or "shield of our fathers," was consecrated in 1878.

8 Telok Ayer Chinese Methodist Church

MAP L5 ■ 235 Telok Ayer St ■ 6324-4001 ■ Open 9am–5pm daily ■ www.tacmc.org.sg

Hokkien Methodists built this church in 1924. Many details, such as the windows and arches, are Roman-style, while the roof line is distinctly traditional Chinese. Services are held in Chinese, Hokkien, and Mandarin dialects.

9 Tan Si Chong Su Temple

MAP K3 ■ 15 Magazine Rd ■ 6533-2880

This shrine is dedicated to the Tan family clan. It was originally built on the riverside, but due to land reclamation, it now lies well away from the

Shrine at Tan Si Chong Su Temple

water's edge. Behind the temple, a private hall encloses ancestral tablets of deceased clan members.

10 Hong San See Temple

MAP J2 ■ 29 Mohammed Sultan Rd ■ 6737-3683

Built on a hill above Mohammed Sultan Road, this 100-year-old temple complex was erected by migrants from the Fujian province in China. Inside the entrance hall are granite plaques listing the donors who contributed to the building. The temple is dedicated to the God of Fortune, the Goddess of Mercy, and the Heavenly Emperor. It was designated as a national monument in Singapore in 1978.

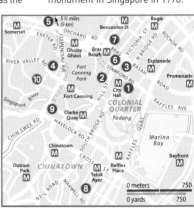

🔟 Architectural Sights

The dome-like structure of the Esplanade with the Singapore Flyer behind

1 Old Parliament House

Singapore's oldest building, dating from 1827, was mistakenly built as a private residence on a spot reserved for government use and subsequently taken over by the colonial administration. Designed by G. D. Coleman, the Neo-Palladian-style building incorporates verandas and high ceilings. In 2003, it was converted to The Arts House, a venue for exhibitions, recitals, and other events (see pp14–15).

2 The Esplanade – Theatres on the Bay

MAP N2–N3 ▪ 1 Esplanade Drive ▪ 6828-8377 ▪ Open 10am–11pm daily ▪ www.esplanade.com

Built at a cost of S$600 million, the Esplanade opened in 2002 amid debate over its aesthetic worth. The aluminum shades encasing its domes inspire locals to call it "the Durian," after the infamous, spiky local fruit.

3 Emerald Hill Road

Pre-war row houses lining this road were some of the earliest to be conserved as private residences. Their architecture illustrates the cultural influences of the 1900s. Houses of note are at numbers 41, 77, and 79–81 (see p95).

4 City Hall and Supreme Court

MAP M2 ▪ 3 St. Andrew's Rd

Both buildings impress from the outside – City Hall with its columns and wide steps, and the old Supreme Court with its dome. The two buildings now form the National Gallery *(see p38)*. Visitors can view the chamber where the Japanese signed their surrender in 1945, as well as the court's marbled corridors and courtrooms.

5 St. Andrew's Cathedral
MAP M2 ■ 11 St. Andrew's Rd ■ 6337-6104 ■ Open 9am–5pm Mon–Sat ■ www.livingstreams.org.sg

Resembling an English parish church, this Anglican church, consecrated in 1862, is made of *chunam*, a paste of shell lime, egg whites, and coarse sugar mixed with boiled coconut husks. The recipe was imported from British India and applied by Indian convict laborers.

6 Empress Place Building
In 1867, the government built the Empress Place to house its administrative offices. Placed at the mouth of the Singapore River, the Neo-Palladian structure was one of the first things newcomers to the city would see on arrival. In the 1980s, it was converted into the Asian Civilisations Museum, its design surviving several major extensions over the years *(see pp14–15)*.

Empress Place Building extension

7 The Istana and Sri Temasek
MAP D3, D4 ■ Orchard Rd ■ Open on select public holidays ■ Adm ■ www.istana.gov.sg

The Istana, which means "palace" in Malay, was built in 1869 as a governor's residence. Situated on a hilltop, it is a blend of traditional Malay palace design and Italian Renaissance decor *(see p94)*.

The colorful exterior of Tan House

8 Tan House
MAP F4 ■ 37 Kerbau Rd ■ No public access

This house, built in 1900, is a mix of cultural influences, with European columns and arched windows, Chinese green tiles, and Malay wooden detailing. It now houses offices.

9 Victoria Theatre and Concert Hall
This ornate structure was built in the Italian Renaissance style popular in Victorian England at the time. The theatre was finished in 1862. In 1905, the Memorial Hall was added to honor Queen Victoria *(see p89)*.

10 CHIJMES (Convent of the Holy Infant Jesus)
MAP M1 ■ 30 Victoria St ■ Open 8am–midnight daily (clubs open till late) ■ www.chijmes.com.sg

This convent was originally built in 1841, and an orphanage was added in 1856. In 1903, a chapel was added, lending a Gothic touch with arches and columns. In 1983, the convent made way for clubs and restaurants.

🔟 World War II Sights

Memorial statue at Bukit Chandu

1 Reflections at Bukit Chandu

MAP S3 ■ 31-K Pepys Rd ■ 6375-2510 ■ Open 9am–5:30pm Tue–Sun ■ Adm

In February 1942, 1,400 soldiers of the Malay Regiment took a stand on Bukit Chandu against 13,000 Japanese soldiers. This museum recounts the battle and the courage displayed by the soldiers.

2 Fort Siloso

The last British coastal fort on Sentosa island offers an insight into the lives of World War II soldiers. The Surrender Chambers recreate the 1945 British and Japanese surrenders (see pp32–3).

3 Labrador Park

MAP S3 ■ Labrador Villa Rd ■ Open 24 hours daily

Guns capable of firing shells almost 10 miles (16 km) were installed at Fort Pasir Panjang to help protect it from attack by sea. Many of the gun emplacements can still be seen.

4 Battle Box

MAP E6 ■ 2 Cox Terrace ■ 6338-6133 ■ Tours compulsory (timetables online) ■ www.battlebox.com.sg

The museum is housed in what was the British World War II command center, which was designed to be bombproof and capable of recycling its air supply. Models depict the 1942 meeting in which General Percival decided to surrender to the Japanese.

5 Changi Chapel and Museum

This museum is dedicated to those held at Changi Prison and camp from 1942 to 1945, and features replicas of the murals painted in St. Luke's Chapel by Bombardier Stanley Warren (see p38).

6 Johore Battery

MAP V2 ■ Cosford Rd ■ 6546-9897 ■ Open 9am–5pm daily

The British guns at Johore were the largest outside the UK when they were installed in 1939 for the defence of Singapore. The originals were destroyed before the fall of Singapore but those have now been replaced with replicas. Tunnels used to store ammunition were discovered here in 1991 by the Singapore Prisons Department.

7 Kranji War Memorial and Cemetery

This memorial stands over the graves of more than 4,000 Allied servicemen lost in battle here. The pillars list the names of 24,000 others whose bodies were not found (see p103).

Kranji War Memorial and Cemetery

The Padang

This is the downtown "playing field" where Japanese troops gathered and divided the European population. British and Australian soldiers were to be held at the Selarang Barracks, while 2,300 civilians were sent to Changi Prison. After the Japanese surrendered to the British, a victory parade was held here.

Pillars at the Civilian War Memorial

 Civilian War Memorial

MAP M2 ■ War Memorial, Beach Rd

Locally known as the "chopsticks," the four pillars here symbolize the races (Chinese, Malay, Indian, and others) that suffered during the Japanese occupation. Remains of unidentified victims are buried at the base of the monument.

Lim Bo Seng Memorial

MAP M3 ■ Queen Elizabeth Walk

This monument is a tribute to local hero Lim Bo Seng, who escaped to Sri Lanka after the Japanese invasion to train resistance fighters. Captured upon his return to the Malay Peninsula, he died in captivity.

MAJOR WORLD WAR II EVENTS IN SINGAPORE

General Percival surrenders

1 December 7–8, 1941
The Japanese attacked Pearl Harbor and then launched a huge offensive, invading the Philippines, Hong Kong, and Thailand, and dropping the first bombs on Singapore.

2 February 8, 1942
Japan invaded Singapore from the north by crossing the causeway.

3 February 15, 1942
British General Percival surrendered to General Yamashito of Japan, and the Japanese occupation began.

4 February 16, 1942
The European population assembled at the Padang, before being marched 14 miles (23 km) to Changi Prison.

5 May 1943
The first group of 600 prisoners was dispatched to work on the notorious Burma-Thailand "death railway."

6 1943
Wartime rations were cut as the war turned against Japan and living conditions began to worsen.

7 November 1944
Starvation and disease were widespread. The US carried out its first raid on the Singapore harbor.

8 Early 1945
Living conditions became almost unbearable, with many people dying of malnutrition and disease.

9 May 1945
News of the end of the European War reached Singapore – the end was near for the desperate city.

10 September 12, 1945
Japan surrendered to Lord Mountbatten, the last British Viceroy of India, in a formal ceremony at Singapore's City Hall.

TOP 10 National Parks and Gardens

1 Singapore Botanic Gardens

Although Orchard Road is just a short walk away, the city seems deceptively distant when you are surrounded by frangipani (plumeria) trees, lakes, and rainforest. A walk through the tranquil gardens is the perfect follow-up to a day of sightseeing or shopping. Locals may be seen practicing Tai Chi on the lawns in the morning (see pp24–5).

2 Chinese and Japanese Gardens

Two unique landscaping philosophies have been used to create a pair of gardens on adjoining islands on Jurong Lake, in the western region of Singapore. The Chinese Garden features an excellent Suzhou-style bonsai collection, colorful buildings, and a stone boat. Steps away, over the Bridge of Double Beauty, the Japanese Garden is the essence of serenity. Enjoy the view of both from the top of the Chinese Garden's seven-story pagoda (see p101).

3 The Southern Ridges

These forested ridges along Singapore's southwest coast comprise four interconnected parks stretching over 6 miles (10 km), linked by pathways and bridges (see p100).

Sungei Buloh Wetland Reserve

4 Sungei Buloh Wetland Reserve

Boardwalk trails wind through this reserve among mangroves that are home to mudskippers and monitor lizards. Look out for the Atlas moth, one of the largest in the world, with a wingspan of up to 1 ft (0.3 m). Hides by the pools allow you to observe some of the 144 bird species found here (see p101).

5 Gardens by the Bay

MAP P4 ■ 18 Marina Gardens Drive ■ Opening time varies ■ 6420-6848 ■ www.gardensbythebay.com.sg

Spanning a huge area, Gardens by the Bay is an award-winning Singapore park, comprising three waterfront gardens – Bay South Garden, Bay East Garden, and Bay Central Garden. The main attraction, Bay South Garden, has popular features such as the Flower Dome, the Cloud Forest, and the Supertree

Gardens by the Bay

Grove. The park also hosts various events and is a popular destination among people of all ages.

6 East Coast Park

MAP T3 ■ East Coast Parkway ■ www.nparks. gov.sg

For many visitors, this park is their first glimpse of Singapore, stretching along the expressway from the airport to the city. The long strip of sandy beach with paths shaded by casuarina trees and coconut palms is popular with bicyclists and roller-bladers. From here, the countless ships plying the Strait make for an incongruous sight.

7 MacRitchie Nature Trail

MAP S2 ■ Off Lornie Rd ■ Open daily ■ www. nparks.gov.sg

Vestiges of the city-state's rubber plantations can be seen from the board-walk encircling this reservoir park. Trails through the forest range in length from 2 to 7 miles (3 to 11 km). The 82-ft- (25-m-) high treetop walk has spectacular views of the forest canopy.

National Orchid Garden

8 National Orchid Garden

One of the highlights of the Botanic Gardens is this collection of over 1,000 orchid species and 2,000 hybrids. Beautifully landscaped, the garden boasts different environ-ments for each group of orchids and bromeliads. The Coolhouse offers a welcome respite from the year-round heat of the city (see pp24–5).

9 Fort Canning Park

This park is inextricably linked with every era of Singapore's history. Originally called "Forbidden Hill," it is said to be the site of the tomb of Iskandar Shah, who first settled Singapore. Raffles built his bungalow here but, in 1859, it was replaced by a military base and renamed Fort Canning. The fort became the British headquarters in the Battle for Singapore. Raffles designated it the island's first botanic garden (see p90–91).

10 Sentosa Nature Walk

Given its short distance and well-graded paths, this walk is one of the easiest ways for children or less-able visitors to glimpse Singapore's forest. However, it is not accessible for strollers and wheelchairs (see pp32–3).

📐 Spas

① Willow Stream Spa
MAP M1 ■ Fairmont Singapore, 80 Bras Basah Rd ■ 6339-7777 ■ Open 7am–10pm daily ■ www.fairmont.com/singapore/willow-stream

This spa is a haven of soft music and earth tones. For a full body-upampering experience, book in for one of the Willow Streams Experiences, such as the Pearl and Cavier body polish, massage, and facial. The East meets West massage utilizes hot volcanic stones and essential oils.

Swimming pool at So SPA by Sofitel

② So SPA by Sofitel
MAP S3 ■ The Sentosa, 2 Bukit Manis Rd ■ 6708-8358 ■ Open 10am–9pm daily (last adm 8pm) ■ www.sofitel-singapore-sentosa.com

Located in the heart of Sentosa Island, this spa is built on a vast 64,580 sq ft (6,000 sq m) heritage site. It has six outdoor pavilions besides 14 indoor treatment rooms. A choice of options allows guests to customize their sessions.

③ Estheva Spa
MAP N2 ■ Level 5, Marina Mandarin Hotel, 6 Raffles Boulevard ■ 6266-6833 ■ Open 10am–10pm daily ■ www.estheva.com

This spa is all about luxury. Try the "choc de-ager" treatment, which includes a chocolate body scrub, a chocolate fondue wrap, and a warm almond oil massage. The treatments combined are said to have four times the antioxidants of tea.

④ Banyan Tree Spa
MAP N4 ■ Level 55, Tower 1, Marina Bay Sands, 10 Bayfront Avenue ■ 6688-8825 ■ Open 10am–11pm Sun-Thu, 10–1am Fri & Sat ■ www.banyantreespa.com

One of the loftiest spas on the island, Banyan Tree has stunning views over the city center. There are traditional Asian massages as well as customized ones, and treatments such as the Royal Banyan, featuring cucumber cleanser, and a blissful herbal bath.

⑤ Damai Spa
MAP B3 ■ Grand Hyatt Singapore, 10 Scotts Rd ■ 6416-7156 ■ Open 10am–10pm daily ■ www.singapore.grand.hyatt.com

Spread over 12,700 sq ft (1,180 sq m), Damai Spa uses Singapore's National Flower, the Vanda Miss Joaquim, as its signature essence. The spa has 11 treatment rooms with special features.

⑥ Spa Esprit at HOUSE
MAP S3 ■ 8D Dempsey Rd ■ 6479-0070 ■ Open 10am–9pm Mon-Sat, 10am–7pm Sun ■ www.dempseyhouse.com

After a long, cramped flight, head to this branch of Spa Esprit for a hot

Nail products at Spa Esprit at HOUSE

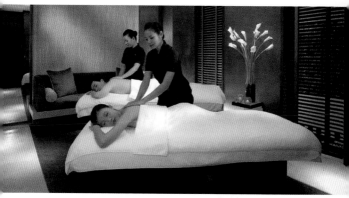

A couple enjoying a massage at The Spa at Mandarin Oriental, Singapore

stone massage. A therapist will soften your muscle tissue with heated stones and ease tight spots with a series of deep, intensive strokes. Emerge relaxed and ready for a drink at the in-house bar.

7 Ikeda Spa Prestige

#05–22 Clark Quay Central, 6 Eu Tong Sen St ▪ 6338-8080 ▪ Open 1–10pm daily ▪ www.ikedaspa.com

The spa recreates the traditional Japanese ryokan bath-house experience in a luxurious style in Singapore. There's a communal bath with mineral-enriched water and a wide range of massages, as well as treatments.

8 ESPA

Resorts World Sentosa, 8 Sentosa Gateway ▪ 6577-8880 ▪ Open 9am–10pm daily ▪ www.rwsentosa.com

With a beach villa and treatment pavilions in its lush gardens, this spacious spa is the perfect oasis for a vacation. All of the treatments and facilities are to a high standard, including the Turkish bath and Japanese hot-spring pools.

9 The Spa at Mandarin Oriental, Singapore

MAP N2 ▪ Mandarin Oriental, Singapore, 5 Raffles Avenue ▪ 6885-3533 ▪ Open 10am–11pm daily ▪ www.mandarinoriental.com/singapore/luxury-spa

This intimate haven of healing, relaxation, and calm has six treatment rooms and offers a range of results-driven therapies.

10 White Panda

148 Arab St ▪ 6292-2148 ▪ Open 11am–4pm daily

Come here for reflexology and traditional Chinese massage, including *tui na* – a deep tissue massage that is also meant to be therapeutic, although some people find it painful.

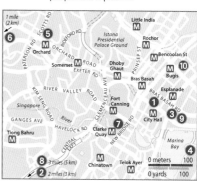

📖10 Off the Beaten Path

as sea kayaking and dragon-boat racing. The state-of-the-art Singapore Sports Hub, on the east bank, comprises the National Stadium and Sports Museum, and has excellent dining for all price budgets. Kallang Riverside Park is a lovely stroll from the Singapore Flyer, along the palm-lined Marina Promenade.

3 Karaoke Nights
www.koshidaka.com.sg/k-suites, www.tendollarclub.sg

Act like a local, and take family and friends for a night's karaoke. Splash cash at exclusive K Suites at Orchard Parade Hotel, with its themed rooms, or go basic at Ten Dollar Club in Chinatown. There are dozens of karaoke bars across the city, but watch out as some can be sleazy. Some stay open until 6am and are good for late-nighters.

1 Black-and-White Houses

Dotted around Singapore are little pockets of colonial-era black-and-white houses, with sweeping grounds and evocative names. Wessex Estate in Queenstown is an ideal place to explore, with Art Deco bungalows and flats, and an artist community. Finish with refreshments in time-warp ColBar, a no-frills eatery that was a military canteen. Nearby Alexandra Park has more grand black-and-white mansions.

2 Kallang River Basin
www.sportshub.com.sg

Kallang River flows into this basin, creating a hub for water sports such

4 St. John's, Lazarus, and Kusu Islands
www.islandcruise.com.sg

Take a picnic to visit these tiny islands off Singapore's south coast. There are white-sand beaches, walking trails, a vibrant Chinese temple, a tortoise sanctuary, and sacred Malay shrines – and on a weekday, they are all blissfully quiet.

Pier on Kusu Island

There are between two and five ferry departures per day, stopping first at larger St. John's, which is connected to Lazarus by a causeway.

5 Changi Point Coastal Walk

Open 24 hours

Stroll east from Changi Point along this boardwalk tracing the coastline, and Singapore will suddenly feel like a sleepy little island. It gives views across the sea to Pulau Ubin and Malaysia, culminating at a sunset spot. It is romantically lit at night, and you will find great food options at Changi Village, near the Point.

6 Everton Road

MAP J5

This charming road and its adjacent streets are pristine examples of colorful Peranakan row houses. Gorgeous nostalgic murals, by local resident Mr. Yip Yew Chong, decorate some of the walls, depicting the Singaporean life of yesteryear. The local coffee shops are highly rated.

A Fleawhere market

7 Flea Markets

www.fleawhere.com

Singapore may be famous for high-end fashion stores and luxury shopping malls, but the city also has a plethora of popular flea markets offering a wide range of crafts, local produce, vintage fashion, and much more. Fleawhere organizes regular markets in varying locations around the city, reportedly every day of the week.

National University of Singapore

8 National University of Singapore and Lee Kong Chian Natural History Museum

The free NUS Museum *(see p54)* has a collection of over 7,000 Southeast Asian artifacts, and changing art and archaeology exhibitions. Also on site is the excellent Lee Kong Chian Natural History Museum *(see p38)* (admission charge), with 20 zones of regional animal specimens and dinosaurs. Although partly interactive, the museum harks back to the days of wooden display cases including cabinets of curiosities.

9 Coney Island Park

www.nparks.gov.sg

Off Singapore's northern coast, this unspoilt casuarina-covered island is connected to the mainland by two bridges. Opened in 2015, there are walking trails, bike tracks, tiny beaches, and a mangrove boardwalk.

10 Punggol Waterway Park

www.nparks.gov.sg

The new town of Punggol is dense with shiny high-rises, but interwoven with a landscaped waterway park and promenade. Impressive bridges, nature, recreation areas, and heritage zones help create a sense of a waterfront town.

⓾ Children's Attractions

perfect for kids. It has an obstacle adventure trail, treehouses, a toddlers' play zone, and inter-active water features. A family-friendly café is on site, too.

④ Singapore Science Centre
MAP R2 ▪ 15 Science Centre Rd ▪ 6425-2500 ▪ Open 10am–6pm daily; Observatory 7:45–10pm Fri ▪ Adm ▪ www.science.edu.sg

The largely interactive exhibits at this remarkable science museum challenge kids to take on subjects as diverse as climate change, optics, ageing, and robotics.

Riding the flumes at Wild Wild Wet

① Wild Wild Wet
MAP U2 ▪ 1 Pasir Ris Close ▪ 6581-9128 ▪ Open 1–7pm Mon–Fri, 10am–7pm weekends & public holidays ▪ Adm ▪ www.wildwildwet.com

Get soaked on the flumes, water mazes, and the Royal Flush – Asia's first hybrid water ride.

② Universal Studios Singapore®
MAP S3 ▪ 8 Sentosa Gateway ▪ 6577-8888 ▪ Open 10am–7pm daily ▪ Adm ▪ www.rwsentosa.com

The biggest draw on Sentosa, this movie-centric theme park features many high-octane rides, Hollywood-style film sets, and more.

③ The Far East Organization's Children's Garden
Open 10am–7pm Tue–Fri, 9am–9pm Sat & Sun

This watery fun garden at Gardens by the Bay is a free attraction that is

⑤ Singapore Discovery Centre
MAP Q2 ▪ 510 Upper Jurong Rd ▪ 6792-6188 ▪ Open 9am–6pm Tue–Sun ▪ Adm ▪ www.sdc.com.sg

This museum, in the west of Singapore, has a militaristic theme, with one section devoted to the Singapore Armed Forces, but there are also exhibits with a futuristic theme, as well as children's movie screenings.

⑥ Snow City
MAP R2 ▪ 21 Jurong Town Hall Rd ▪ 6560-2306 ▪ Open 10am–6pm daily (last adm 5pm) ▪ Adm ▪ www.snowcity.com.sg

Board or ski at Snow City, while children build snowmen or check out the igloo in the play area. The temperature is maintained at -5° C (23° F), so dress warmly. Coats and boots can be rented on site.

Universal Studios Singapore®

7 Jurong Bird Park

This is one of the largest parks of its kind. An overhead railroad runs through the Waterfall Aviary, featuring the world's tallest man-made waterfall *(see p101)*.

8 Adventure Cove Waterpark

MAP S3 ▪ 8 Sentosa Gateway ▪ 6577-8888 ▪ Open 10am–6pm daily ▪ Adm ▪ www.rwsentosa.com

High-speed water slides, snorkeling above a tropical reef, and tubing down Adventure River are among the attractions here.

9 Live Turtle and Tortoise Museum

MAP R2 ▪ 1 Chinese Garden Rd ▪ 6268-5363 ▪ Open 10am–7pm daily ▪ Adm ▪ www.turtle-tortoise.com

Located in the Chinese Gardens, this miniature zoo has over 200 turtles and tortoises from over 60 species, some of which wander freely around.

10 S.E.A. Aquarium

MAP S3 ▪ 8 Sentosa Gateway ▪ 6577-8888 ▪ Open 10am–6pm daily ▪ Adm ▪ www.rwsentosa.com

With ten different zones, including the Shark Seas, this aquarium mesmerizes everyone through close-up encounters with marine life.

Fish tank at S.E.A Aquarium

TOP 10 SPORTS

Sea canoeing in East Coast Park

1 Golf
MAP T3 ▪ 80 Rhu Cross ▪ 6348-1923
Just east of the center of the city, the 18-hole Marina Bay Golf Course is open to the public and has great views.

2 Sea Canoeing
Kayaks and canoes can be rented in Sentosa or at East Coast Park *(see p47)*.

3 Water-Skiing
MAP U2 ▪ 1206A East Coast Parkway ▪ 6636-4266
The Singapore Wake Park tows skiers and wakeboarders around a cableway.

4 Windsurfing
MAP T3 ▪ 1390 East Coast Parkway ▪ 6444-0409
Water-Venture at East Coast Park offers both instruction and equipment.

5 Sailing
MAP U2 ▪ 1500 East Coast Parkway ▪ 6444-4555
The Singapore Sailing Federation runs courses for all ages.

6 Swimming
MAP T2 ▪ 100 Tyrwhitt Rd ▪ 6293-9058
The Jalan Besar Swimming Complex is the most centrally located of the island's numerous Olympic-sized pools, with only nominal admission fees.

7 Hiking
Hike through rainforest at Bukit Timah *(see p101–03)* and MacRitchie *(see p47)*.

8 Biking
Bikes can be rented at East Coast Park, Sentosa, and Pulau Ubin *(see pp46–7 and p51)*.

9 Rollerblading
East Coast Park is superb for rollerblading, and has several rental shops.

10 Beach Volleyball
Siloso Beach has four popular courts, so go early at weekends *(see pp32–3)*.

🔟 Arts Venues

The colorful Artrium@MCI

① Artrium@MCI
MAP L2 ▪ 140 Hill St ▪ www.artriumatmci.sg

Clustered in the lobby of the Ministry of Communications and Information (MCI) building, a group of private art galleries sells contemporary works from Asia's top artists, primarily from India, China, and Southeast Asia. Notable galleries include Art-2.

② NUS Museum
50 Kent Ridge Crescent, National University of Singapore ▪ 6516-8817 ▪ Open 10am–6pm Tue–Sun ▪ www.museum.nus.edu.sg

The university's museum displays Southeast Asian and Chinese art, including brush paintings and porcelain. It also hosts permanent and temporary exhibitions of modern art, a constant fixture being the sculptures and ceramics of a home-grown modern master, Ng Eng Teng.

③ Singapore Tyler Print Institute
MAP J2 ▪ 41 Robertson Quay ▪ 6336-3663 ▪ Open 10am–7pm Mon–Fri, 9am–6pm Sat ▪ www.stpi.com.sg

Established in 2002, this institute works with international artists to create outstanding prints and to explore the technical and creative aspects of print and paper-making. It is housed in a 19th-century warehouse where artists can create, exhibit, and sell their work.

④ Gillman Barracks
MAP S3 ▪ 9 Lock Rd ▪ Open Tue–Sun ▪ www.gillmanbarracks.com

Occupying a former British army barracks built in the 1936, this cluster of galleries showcases modern Southeast Asian and international artists. The on-site Centre for Contemporary Art also offers exhibitions and lectures.

⑤ The Esplanade – Theatres on the Bay
This iconic landmark of Singapore, built as a center for the performing arts, houses two indoor stages (a concert hall and a smaller recital studio) for music, theater, and dance performances by both international and local groups. There is an outdoor stage beside Marina Bay (see p42).

The Esplanade – Theatres on the Bay

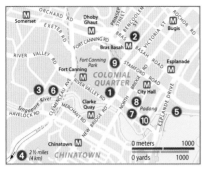

8 National Gallery Singapore

A lavish bid to create a world-class art museum, the National Gallery displays Singaporean and Malayan art in its City Hall wing, plus works from elsewhere in Southeast Asia in the former Supreme Court. There are regular talks, workshops, volunteer-led tours, and other events *(see p38)*.

6 DBS Arts Centre
MAP J2 ▪ 20 Merbau Rd, Robertson Quay ▪ 6733-0005 ▪ www.srt.com.sg

Home to the award-winning Singapore Repertory Theatre – one of Asia's leading English language theater companies – DBS is located amid dining and nightlife venues. The Little Company hosts performances for children here.

7 The Arts House at Old Parliament House

Rooms that were once used for parliamentary discussions now welcome music and dance performances, poetry readings, lectures, screenings, and other fringe events. The old rooms are intimate, with hardwood floors, decorative molding, and special fixtures, all intact. The building also has a café and pub *(see pp14–15)*.

National Gallery Singapore

9 The Substation
MAP L1 ▪ 45 Armenian St ▪ 6337-7535 ▪ www.substation.org

Singapore's first home for the city's independent artists has a black box theater, a gallery, and multipurpose rooms. These host diverse events from indie gigs to film festivals.

10 Victoria Theatre and Concert Hall

Though home to the Singapore Symphony Orchestra, this concert hall stages other performances as well. The details of this revamped, ornate building are as much a part of the performance as the music itself *(see p89)*.

🔟 Bars and Lounges

SkyBar at CÉ LA VI has views across the Singapore skyline

1 CÉ LA VI
MAP N4 ▪ 1 Bayfront Avenue, Sands SkyPark, Marina Bay Sands ▪ 6508-2188 ▪ Open noon–late daily

Boasting a stunning location on top of Marina Bay Sands, this must-visit venue features the alfresco SkyBar. A multitiered restaurant serves Modern Asian cuisine, and there is also a chic nightclub.

2 Harry's, Dempsey Hill
MAP S3 ▪ Block 11, Dempsey Rd ▪ 6471-9018 ▪ Open 4pm–1 or 2am Mon–Fri, noon–1 or 2am Sat & Sun

Part of the Harry's chain, this unpretentious lounge can be found among the community of galleries, restaurants, and pubs on Dempsey Hill. It is a laid-back place with sofas and low tables. Happy hour runs until 8pm, and there is live evening music on Thursdays and Fridays.

3 Crazy Elephant
MAP K2 ▪ Clarke Quay ▪ 6337-7859 ▪ Open 5pm–2 or 3am daily

Local and visiting musicians play rock 'n' roll and blues here every night. With a focus on music and beer, Crazy Elephant is a more casual option than other bars in the area. There is outside seating overlooking the river.

4 No. 5, Emerald Hill
MAP C5 ▪ 5 Emerald Hill ▪ 6732-0818 ▪ Open noon–2 or 3am Mon–Sat, 5pm–2am Sun

In a restored 1910 Peranakan shophouse just off Orchard Road, No. 5 has a location, cocktail list, and buzzy ambience that all appeal to the expatriate crowd. During the day, it's quieter and easier to admire the Chinese teak carving and opium beds at the back.

5 Acid Bar
MAP C5 ▪ Peranakan Place, #01–01/02, 180 Orchard Rd ▪ 6732-6966 ▪ Open 5pm–2am Sun–Thu, 5pm–3am Fri & Sat ▪ No cover charge

The central location draws in crowds for live music, and the dance floor stays rowdy until late. Weekdays are more relaxed, with happy-hour drinks.

Cocktail, Acid Bar

6 Muddy Murphy's Irish Pub
MAP A3 ▪ 442 Orchard Rd ▪ 6735-0400 ▪ Open 11am–1 or 2am daily

When the urge for a Guinness is irresistible, this friendly pub delivers more than most Irish bars. Despite a basement address, it offers an outdoor seating area. Inside, a big-screen TV shows live sports. There is live music on weekends.

7 The Rabbit Hole
MAP S5 ▪ 39C Harding Rd
▪ 6473-9965 ▪ Open 6–11:30pm Tue–Thu & Sun, 6pm–12:30am Fri & Sat

Housed in a restored colonial-era chapel, this bar specializes in gin. Also on offer is a range of French sweet crepes.

8 Loof
MAP M1 ▪ 331 North Bridge Rd, #03–07 Odeon Towers Extension Rooftop ▪ 6337-9416 ▪ Open 5pm–1am Mon–Thu, 5pm–3am Fri & Sat

Singapore's first standalone rooftop bar is renowned for its quirky character. People come here to sip Southeast Asian-inspired cocktails – like Kaya Lumpur or bubble tea with orange liqueur – and for a food menu that is packed with distinctive local flavors.

Chic modern interior at Loof

9 1-Altitude
MAP L4 ▪ Level 61–63, 1 Raffles Place ▪ 6438-0410 ▪ Open 6pm–2am Sun–Tue, until 4am Wed, Fri, & Sat, until 3am Thu

Claimed to be the world's loftiest rooftop bar, 1-Altitude is actually higher up than Singapore's highest peak, Bukit Timah. Stunning views in all directions handsomely repay the stiff cover charge.

10 Harry's Bar, Boat Quay
MAP L3 ▪ 28 Boat Quay ▪ 6538-3029 ▪ Open 11–1am Sun–Thu, 11–2am Fri, Sat, & eve of public hols

Popular with tourists and banking executives, this riverside bar has alfresco seating and live sports.

TOP 10 NIGHTCLUBS AND DISCOS

1 Zouk
The Cannery, 3C River Valley Rd
▪ 6738-2988
Located within a sizeable space at Clarke Quay, Singapore's flagship club now has four venues under one roof.

2 CÉ LA VI Club Lounge
MAP N4 ▪ North SkyPark, Marina Bay Sands
Nightly DJ sets and staggering views from the 57th floor.

3 Headquarters by The Council
MAP L3 ▪ Level 2, 66 Boat Quay
Genuinely underground scene for house, techno, and "alt dance" genres.

4 Canvas
MAP L3 ▪ 20 Upper Circular Rd, B1–01/06, The Riverwalk ▪ 9169-3815
Built in collaboration with Home Club, Canvas is a blend of a nightclub, a lounge, and an art gallery.

5 Cherry Discotheque
21 Mount Elizabeth ▪ 9760-3031
Hip-hop, grime, and other cutting edge sounds at this venue nestled in the basement of the York Hotel.

6 Attica
MAP K2 ▪ 3A River Valley Rd, #01–03 Clarke Quay ▪ 6333-9973
Lounge, mingle, spot celebrities, and dance at this club with four areas.

7 Altimate
MAP J2 ▪ 1 Raffles Place #61
▪ 6438-0410
This VIP venue on 61st floor commands a pricey cover charge.

8 Refuge
MAP M1 ▪ B01-03 CHIJMES, 30 Victoria St
Chilled out, soulful sounds amid the salubrious setting of CHIJMES (See p43).

9 Tanjong Beach Club
120 Tanjong Beach Walk, Sentosa
▪ 6270-1355
Party to house and other sounds by the seaside at the beach parties here, staged at least monthly.

10 Space Club
MAP N3 ▪ #01–03 Magazine Rd
▪ 6443-4500
Enjoy electric dance and pop music, resident DJs, and insane LED displays. Ladies' night is on Wednesdays.

🔟 Restaurants

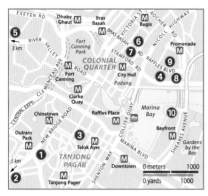

It has an extensive wine list and is known for the large number of working professionals it attracts.

4 Morton's of Chicago
MAP N2 ■ Mandarin Oriental Hotel, 5 Raffles Avenue ■ 6339-3740 ■ Open 5:30–11pm Mon–Sat, noon–3pm & 5–9pm Sun ■ Reservations advisable ■ $$$

Ebullient waiters at this upmarket steakhouse follow the menu with an immense platter, heaving with sample cuts of beef or vegetables. The seafood competes with superbly fresh lobsters, oysters, and shrimp.

1 Majestic Restaurant
MAP J5 ■ 31–7 Bukit Pasoh Rd ■ 6511-4718 ■ Open 11:45am–3pm & 6–10pm daily ■ www.restaurantmajestic.com ■ $$$

Beautifully presented, modern Cantonese dishes are served in this stylish restaurant in the heart of Chinatown. Specialties include Chinese-style honey lamb chops and noodles with Boston lobster.

5 The White Rabbit
39C Harding Rd ■ 6473-9965 ■ Open noon–2:30pm Tue–Fri, 10:30am–3pm Sat–Sun, 6:30–10:30pm Tue–Sun ■ www.whiterabbit.com.sg ■ $$

Set in a restored chapel and worth a visit for the architecture alone, The White Rabbit serves delicious European cuisine with Asian touches.

2 TungLok Heen
MAP S3 ■ Lobby Level, Hotel Michael, Resort World Sentosa ■ 6884-7888 ■ Open 11:30am–2:30pm & 6:30–10:30pm daily ■ www.tunglokheen.com ■ $$$

The perfect retreat for those who appreciate traditional and authentic Chinese cuisine. The menu includes an array of fresh Teochew delights and fiery Hunan cuisine besides celebrity chef Susur Lee's signature creations, such as roast Irish duck.

The White Rabbit's unusual interior

3 IndoChine @ Club Street
MAP K4 ■ 47 Club Street, Chinatown ■ 6323-0503 ■ Open noon–10:30pm Mon–Fri, 6–10:30pm Sat ■ www.indochine-group.com ■ $$$

A veteran branch of an established chain, this restaurant specializes in Indochinese cuisine, including Vietnamese, Laotian, and Cambodian.

The Ritz-Carlton's Summer Pavilion, offering fine Cantonese cuisine

6 Raffles Grill

MAP M1 ■ Raffles Hotel, 1 Beach Rd ■ 6412-1816 ■ Open noon–2pm & 7–10pm Mon–Sat, noon–3pm & 7:30–10pm Sun ■ Reservations recommended ■ www.raffleshotel.com ■ $$$

Raffles Hotel's most formal and elegant dining room serves international cuisine. The menu changes every season, but past favorites have included a delicate Dover sole, as well as tender beef tenderloin.

7 Mikuni

MAP M1–M2 ■ Level 3, Fairmont Singapore, 80 Bras Basah Rd ■ 6431-6156 ■ Open noon–2:30pm & 6:30–10:30pm ■ www.fairmont.com ■ $$$

With a modern approach to Japanese cuisine, Mikuni offers a *robatayaki* grilling counter, sushi and teppanyaki stations.

Quail sausage, Raffles Grill

8 Summer Pavilion

MAP N2 ■ Ritz-Carlton Millenia, 7 Raffles Avenue ■ 6434-5286 ■ Open 11:30am–2:30pm & 6:30–10:30pm daily ■ www.ritzcarlton.com ■ $$$

The Ritz-Carlton's swankiest restaurant serves top-class Cantonese food. The dim sum and lobster noodles are extremely popular. Set lunches are good value.

9 Rang Mahal

MAP N2 ■ Level 3, Pan Pacific Hotel, 7 Raffles Boulevard ■ 6333-1788 ■ Open noon–2:30pm Sun–Fri, 6:30–10:30pm daily ■ www.rangmahal.com.sg ■ $$$

In business since 1971, this restaurant is renowned for its pursuit of excellence. Expect a range of cuisines from the northern, coastal, and southern regions of India, all complemented by an expansive wine list.

10 CUT

MAP P4 ■ Galleria Level, The Shoppes at Marina Bay Sands ■ 6688-8517 ■ Open 5:30–10pm daily (to 11pm Fri & Sat); Bar & Lounge: 5:30pm–midnight daily ■ www.marinabaysands.com ■ $$$

Celebrity chef Wolfgang Puck's first Asian venture puts a contemporary twist on the classic steakhouse menu. As well as the finest cuts of beef, diners here will find a fabulous cellar and impeccable service.

For a key to restaurant price ranges see p75

TOP 10 Hawker Centers and Food Courts

Maxwell Food Centre

1 Maxwell Food Centre

MAP K5 ▪ Corner of South Bridge Rd & Maxwell Rd ▪ Open 8am–10pm daily

A Chinatown favorite, this hawker center has an extensive menu of Chinese favorites, usually served with rice. Try the famous Hainanese chicken at Tian Tian Hainanese Chicken Rice stall.

2 Chinatown Food Street

MAP K6 ▪ Smith St ▪ Open 6–11pm daily

This pedestrianized street is lined with touristy food kiosks decorated to look like the push-carts hawkers used in bygone days. The Boon Tat Street Barbecued Seafood is very good.

Chinatown Food Street

3 Tiong Bahru Food Centre

MAP T3 ▪ 83 Seng Poh Rd ▪ Open 6am–11pm daily

Located in hip Tiong Bahru, one of Singapore's oldest public housing estates, this food center has over 80 stalls. The emphasis is on Chinese fare such as Hainanese chicken rice, roast pork, and fishball noodles. It is busiest and best in the mornings.

4 Chomp Chomp

MAP T2 ▪ 20 Kensington Park ▪ Open 11am–3am daily

A famous suburban hawker center, Chomp Chomp serves excellent barbecued seafood in its relaxed garden setting. There is a good fried carrot cake stall, too.

5 East Coast Lagoon Food Village

MAP U2 ▪ 1220 East Coast Park Service Rd ▪ Open 11am–11pm daily

Ocean breezes keep eating areas cool at this center beside the sea. Find good barbecued seafood at Leng Heng, laksa soup at Roxy, and satay at Haron 30.

6 Tekka Market

MAP F3 ▪ 665 Buffalo Rd ▪ Open 8am–11pm daily

This popular hawker center is good for local Indian fare such as spicy

fried noodles, fish-head curry, and *rojak* (fritters with a sweet chili dip). Also here is one of Singapore's largest wet markets. Busiest in the morning, it sells meat, seafood, vegetables, and tropical fruit.

7 Food Republic
Wisma Atria: MAP B4 ▪ 435 Orchard Rd ▪ Suntec City Mall: MAP P2 ▪ Temasek Ave ▪ VivoCity: *see p62*

This mall food court chain offers a slick take on the traditional hawker center. The VivoCity outlet has the look of a village from yesteryear.

Lau Pa Sat Festival Market

8 Lau Pa Sat Festival Market
MAP M4 ▪ 18 Raffles Quay ▪ Open 11am–3am daily

In the heart of the banking district, this hawker center features Victorian cast-iron architecture and a good range of stalls. It is usually packed at lunchtime; in the evening, satay stalls outside are worth a visit.

9 Chinatown Complex
MAP K4 ▪ Block 335 Smith St ▪ Open 11am–11pm daily

This hawker center is known for Chinese food. Try offerings like local-style savory carrot cake, claypot rice, and dumplings.

10 Makansutra Glutton's Bay
MAP N2 ▪ 8 Raffles Avenue ▪ Open 6pm–3am daily

Good for late snacking, this very popular waterfront place offers a reasonable selection of food, including barbecued chicken wings.

TOP 10 LOCAL DISHES

Chicken satay and peanut sauce

1 Laksa
Rice noodles, prawns, and fishcakes come together in a rich soup made from coconut curry, topped with chili and laksa leaf – a local herb.

2 Kaya Toast
A sweet jam made from coconut milk and egg is spread on toast and eaten for breakfast or as a snack.

3 Chili Crab
Whole crab smothered in a sweet and sour, spicy sauce, served with buns for dipping in the sauce.

4 Fish Head Curry
An entire fish head stewed in spicy curry – the cheek meat is said to be the sweetest of the whole animal.

5 Banana Leaf
Southern Indian meal of white rice, vegetable curries, and relish served on a flat banana leaf.

6 Nasi Padang
Indonesian or Malay cooked dishes, such as beef *rendang* or assam (tamarind) fish, served over white rice.

7 Satay
Small skewers of barbecued meats – chicken, beef, mutton – dipped in a sweet peanut and chili sauce.

8 Chicken Rice
Poached or roasted, chopped chicken served over rice that has been cooked in chicken stock.

9 Roti Prata
Indian griddle bread, sometimes containing egg, onion, or even cheese, and served with a curry dip.

10 Chendol
Dessert made of green jelly noodles, sweet beans, brown sugar, coconut milk, and shaved ice.

🔟 Shopping Malls

1 VivoCity
MAP S3 ■ 1 Harbourfront Walk ■ 6377-6870 ■ Open 10am–10pm daily

Singapore's biggest mall also has some of its best views, with platforms overlooking the cable cars swinging over to Sentosa. VivoCity is well designed and airy with great facilities, including food courts and restaurants, a multiplex cinema, and a children's playground.

Outdoor plaza at Ngee Ann City

2 Ngee Ann City
This marble monolith is often known by the name of its main tenant, Takashimaya. The Japanese store rubs shoulders with luxury names, such as Louis Vuitton, Chanel, and Tiffany. Fashion clothing chains include Zara and Dior. Bibliophiles should visit Kinokuniya, Singapore's largest bookstore (see p98).

3 Tanglin Shopping Centre
MAP A4 ■ 19 Tanglin Rd ■ 6737-0849 ■ Open 10am–10pm daily

Not to be confused with Tanglin Mall, this place is a chance to escape familiar global brands and browse antiques, jewelry, and art in a relaxed atmosphere. The old-fashioned mall has a fine selection of traditional and modern Asian furniture, as well as hand-woven carpets and Middle Eastern collectables.

4 Plaza Singapura
MAP E5 ■ 68 Orchard Rd ■ Open 10am–10pm daily

Plaza Singapura has stood the test of time, and remains popular by offering a wide range of good-value products, including clothing, musical instruments, and household items. There's a Marks & Spencer department store and many restaurants.

5 Far East Plaza
MAP B4 ■ 330 Orchard Rd ■ 6734-2325 ■ Open 10am–10pm daily

There are more than 800 stores in this bustling complex. The Plaza is crowded and shabby but presents a different side of Orchard Road. Lower floors have street fashion and local designers; upstairs are tailors, hairdressers, and tattoo parlors.

6 The Shoppes at Marina Bay Sands
MAP N4 ■ 10 Bayfront Ave ■ 6688-8868 ■ Open 10:30am–11pm Sun–Thu, 10:30am–11:30pm Fri–Sat

This vast luxury mall has over 300 stores featuring all the high-end designers. Sampans cruise along a canal at basement level, and there is an observation deck on the roof. Celebrity chef restaurants, trendy café-bars, and a food court provide a break from shopping.

The Shoppes at Marina Bay Sands

Paragon shopping center

⑦ Paragon
MAP C4 ■ 290 Orchard Rd
■ 6738-5535 ■ Open 10am–10pm daily

Exclusivity is the name of the game on Paragon's glamorous ground level, where designer boutiques such as Prada, Balenciaga, and Armani are located. The five other floors have more mainstream designers.

⑧ People's Park Complex
This is one of a couple of 1970s concrete high-rise shopping arcades where ordinary people come to buy ordinary things. It houses the Overseas Emporium, selling mainly Chinese-made goods, plus some shops selling Chinese jade and handicrafts (see p71).

⑨ Raffles City Shopping Centre
MAP M2 ■ 252 North Bridge Rd
■ 6318-0238 ■ Open 10am–9:30pm daily

This center of interlinking malls joins the Stamford and Fairmont hotels with City Hall MRT, the CityLink, and Marina Square. It's home to a branch of Robinsons, Singapore's oldest department store.

⑩ ION Orchard
MAP B4 ■ 2 Orchard Turn
■ 6238-8228 ■ Open 10am–10pm daily

You'll find dozens of high-end fashion and accessories shops, an art gallery, and a basement food hall at this high-rise mall, along with an observation deck that has panoramic views.

TOP 10 LOCAL BUYS

1 Jade
For fixed prices on luminescent green jade jewellery, head to Yue Hwa Chinese Emporium (see p76).

2 Bak kwa
Chewy marinated barbecued pork slices, this portable snack is easily available throughout Chinatown.

3 Chinese Tea
Tea Chapter: 9 & 11 Neil Rd
■ 6226-3026 ■ Open 10:30am–10.30pm ■ www.teachapter.com
Quality teas packaged in attractive tins can be found on Neil Road.

4 Asian Art and Antiques
Best sourced at Tanglin Shopping Centre or Dempsey Hill.

5 Laksa Paste
This is the base for an authentic laksa soup (see p61). Jars of paste can be found in supermarkets island-wide.

6 Peranakan Porcelain
Rumah Bebe: 113 East Coast Rd
■ 6247-8781 ■ Open 9.30am–6.30pm Tue–Sun ■ www.rumahbebe.com
Plates, tea sets, and spoons in various vibrant floral designs.

7 Tiger Balm
Formulated in the 1870s, this herbal ointment soothes aches and repels mosquitoes. Available at pharmacies.

8 Batik
Sarongs, shirts, and fabrics with Malay and Indonesian designs are best bought in Kampong Glam.

9 Kaya Jam
Recreate kaya toast, the national breakfast, with a jar of coconut jam, available at supermarkets.

10 Chinese Seals
Hand-carved personalised Chinese "chops" (seals) in various materials are easy to find in Chinatown's shops.

Batik sarong design

Singapore for Free

The Garden Rhapsody sound-and-light show at the Gardens by the Bay

1 Wonder Full Light and Sound Show

MAP N4 ▪ Marina Bay Sands ▪ Shows at 8pm & 9:30pm daily, 11pm Fri–Sat

Every evening, shows mesmerize viewers at Marina Bay Sands with orchestral music, multicolored strobes, and lovely choreographed fountains. The laser lights can be seen from the Padang and Esplanade too, while the water effects and fountain are best seen from the Events Plaza.

2 Esplanade – Theatres on the Bay

Most weekends feature a free performance here, usually on the Outdoor Stage. The Beautiful Sunday series, held once a month, show-cases local music groups in the spectacular Concert Hall. Exhibition spaces, the library, rooftop terrace, and children's PLAYbox are also freely accessible (see p42).

3 Baba House

MAP T3 ▪ 157 Neil Rd ▪ 6227-5731 ▪ Advance registration required ▪ www.nus.edu.sg/cfa/museum/mission.php

Dating to the 1890s, this indigo-blue Peranakan house offers free one-hour guided tours, five times a week. Beautiful period features and original antiques reveal the life of a wealthy Straits-Chinese family 100 years ago.

4 Gardens by the Bay

Garden Rhapsody show at 7:45pm & 8:45pm

Although there's a charge to enter the conservatories and SkyWalk, the rest of these world-famous gardens are free. Each night the music-and-light Garden Rhapsody show at the Supertree Grove wows visitors (see pp46–7).

5 Sikh Gurdwaras

The British East India Company brought Sikh sepoys to Singapore to be policemen in the 1800s, and the community now numbers around 13,000. In keeping with the ideology, visitors are made welcome at the seven gurdwaras (temples) in the city. Volunteer staff might offer tours, and the langars (communal kitchens) serve free, simple food and masala tea to all.

6 Free Art Tours

The 12 galleries at Gillman Barracks (see p54) are free to explore, and once a month you can register for a free art, history, and heritage tour of the colonial site. Some hotels, including Marina Bay Sands, the Hilton, and Pan Pacific, also have art collections in their public areas.

Concerts in the Park
www.nparks.gov.sg/
concertseries

Free concerts are hosted in parks and gardens across the city. The premier spot is the Symphony Stage in the Botanic Gardens. Set on a lake among water lilies, you may catch the Singapore Symphony Orchestra or an international act here.

Wak Hai Cheng Bio Temple

A Taoist center for the Teochew community, this small temple has a magical feel. Inside the courtyard sit rows of spiral joss sticks, while the temple itself, with its roof covered with restored ceramic figurines, is juxtaposed against the soaring glass-and-steel skyscrapers surrounding it.

Wak Hai Cheng Bio Temple

Hay Dairies

MAP R1 ■ 3 Lim Chu Kang Lane 4 ■ 6792-0931 ■ Open 9am–4pm Wed–Mon ■ www.haydairies.com.sg

There is no charge to visit this small dairy farm, where you can pet the goats. Visiting at milking time is best, from 9am to 10:30am. It is in the Kranji Countryside, where many agri-businesses and farms can be visited – all connected by a bus service.

National Library

MAP M1 ■ 100 Victoria St ■ Open 10am–9pm daily ■ www.nlb.gov.sg

The gleaming 16-floor central library is an award-winning example of "green" architecture. Regularly changing art, photography, and cultural exhibitions are free to visit.

Hop-on hop-off tour bus

🔟 Religious Celebrations

① Chinese New Year
January or February

Singapore's most important public holiday is celebrated in January or February. Celebrations begin on the eve of the holiday, with families gathering for dinner. People visit friends and family, and *hong bao* (red packets containing money) are given to kids.

Chinese New Year gifts

Performers at Chingay Parade

② Chingay Parade
January or February

This ticketed Chinese New Year parade features dance, music, and acrobatics as well as floats. More than 10,000 people take part, with troupes from all over the world adding a multicultural aspect.

③ Thaipusam
January or February

In January or February, this day of thanksgiving sees Hindus honor Lord Muruga. A parade begins at Sri Srinivasa Perumal Temple *(see p79)* and ends at Sri Thendayuthapani Temple *(see p40)*. Many devotees carry heavy *kavadis* (metal racks with fruits and flowers), pierce their tongues and cheeks, and dig hooks into their backs.

④ Hungry Ghost Festival
July or August

The Chinese believe that menacing spirits wander the earth in August and September. To appease these spirits, they offer food, burn joss sticks and "hell money," and stage Chinese operas. New ventures, such as marriages and business openings, are suspended during this inauspicious time.

⑤ Mid-Autumn Festival
September or October

Also called the Lantern Festival, this event celebrates the harvest with mooncakes stuffed with sweet lotus paste, egg, and other fillings.

Mid-Autumn Festival celebrations

Hari Raya Puasa

Ramadan, the Muslim month of fasting, culminates with Hari Raya Puasa, and is celebrated with family and friends. Non-Muslims are often invited to feasts in private homes. The dates change every year.

Preparing the fire-walk for Thimithi

 ## Thimithi
October or November

Each year, in October or November, a procession of Hindus makes its way from Little India's Sri Srinivasa Perumal Temple to the Sri Mariamman Temple *(see p71)*.

 ## Deepavali (Diwali)
October

This Hindu festival marks the triumph of good over evil. Hundreds of oil lamps are lit to guide the souls of the departed back to the afterlife.

 ## Nine Emperor Gods
October

Taoists believe that the Nine Emperor Gods visit earth for nine days in November to care for the sick and bring good luck to the living. Priests in Chinese temples chant, and spirit guides write charms in blood.

 ## Christmas
December

The city keeps the Christmas spirit alive with spectacular decorations along Orchard Road *(see pp94–9)*.

TOP 10 SPORTING AND CULTURAL EVENTS

1 World Gourmet Summit
April sees Singapore host a festival of fine dining, with demonstrations by international celebrity chefs.

2 Singapore International Festival of the Arts
This annual arts festival, held mostly in July and August, draws performers from around the world and spans genres such as theater, dance, and music.

3 Dragon Boat Festival
International teams race dragon boats at the Bedok Reservoir in June.

4 Great Singapore Sale
For six weeks in June and July, local retailers offer excellent discounts.

5 Singapore Food Festival
This month-long celebration of local food, including tours and classes, is held across the city every July.

6 Ballet Under the Stars
This casual event is held at various outdoor venues across the city every July. Perfect for a cultural evening.

7 National Day, August 9
A huge show marks the day Singapore became a nation. Tickets are only available via a public lottery.

8 Formula 1 Singapore Grand Prix
Held each year in September, this is the first night-time race in Grand Prix history and Asia's first to be held on city streets.

9 Singapore Art Week
Visual art comes to the fore every January with two weeks of special art talks, exhibition launches, and the like.

10 Singapore International Film Festival
Some 300 independent films are shown in November and December, with a special focus on Asian cinema.

National Day, August 9

Singapore
Area by Area

Raffles' Landing Site in
the Colonial District

🔟 Chinatown

In 1822, Sir Stamford Raffles laid out a plan that divided Singapore into clearly defined quarters. At the time, the area south of the Singapore River was developing fast, with godowns (warehouses) and shipping offices opening up, and Chinese laborers living in cramped conditions behind them. Chinese temples sprang up alongside clan associations: groups of Chinese who had a common dialect, name, or similar origins. Indian workers also lived here, especially after the opening of the port at Tanjong Pagar in the mid-1800s. Taoist and Hindu temples, churches, and mosques stand side by side, typifying the multicultural spirit of the city.

Buddha Tooth Relic Temple

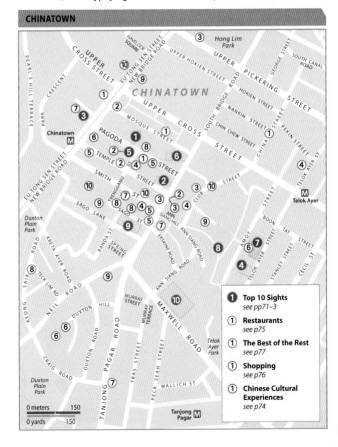

CHINATOWN

- **1** Top 10 Sights
  see pp71–3
- **1** Restaurants
  see p75
- **1** The Best of the Rest
  see p77
- **1** Shopping
  see p76
- **1** Chinese Cultural Experiences
  see p74

0 meters 150
0 yards 150

Chinatown Heritage Centre exhibit

1 Chinatown Heritage Centre

MAP K4 ▪ 48 Pagoda St ▪ 6224-3928 ▪ Open 9am–8pm daily ▪ www.china townheritagecentre.com.sg ▪ Adm

This museum, located in three restored shophouses in the heart of Chinatown, illustrates the harsh conditions in which the Chinese community lived and worked in Singapore's early days. Occupying three levels, it re-creates scenes from old shops, coffee shops, and living cubicles, with an interesting exhibit dedicated to the "four evils" of gambling, opium smoking, prostitution, and secret societies.

2 Sri Mariamman Temple

MAP K4 ▪ 244 South Bridge Rd ▪ 6223-4064 ▪ Open 7am–noon & 6–9pm daily ▪ www.smt.org.sg

Sri Mariamman, or "Mother Goddess" as she is known to Hindus, is honored at this temple, Singapore's oldest Hindu place of worship. It was established in 1823 by Narayana Pillay, a government clerk who arrived aboard Raffles' ship. The current temple was built in 1843 by former Indian convicts. Sri Mariamman is believed to cure diseases, so, appropriately, free medical services are available here.

3 People's Park Complex

MAP K4 ▪ 1 Park Rd ▪ Open 8am–late daily ▪ www.peoplespark complex.sg

This towering concrete block was a ground-breaking development when it was built in the 1970s. The central mall is thick with travel agents, electronics shops, Chinese souvenirs, massage specialists, and beauty therapists. Spilling out at ground level around the mall are kiosks selling intriguing local snacks and money changers offering decent rates. The adjacent People's Park Complex Food Centre has dozens of hawker stands, and is justifiably packed day and night.

4 Al-Abrar Mosque

MAP L5 ▪ 192 Telok Ayer St ▪ 6220-6306 ▪ Open 11:30am–9pm Sat–Thu, 10am–9pm Fri

Once the island's most important mosque, Al-Abrar was originally a seaside hut built from wood and *attap* (thatch). It served the community living and working in the area – hence its name "Koochoo Palli," or "small hut house." Squeezed between shop-houses, with its facade blending in with the city, it is very quiet. It serves a handful of local workers, as most Muslims prefer to pray at mosques closer to home.

Sri Mariamman Temple exterior

Visitors throng the food stalls and shops of the Chinatown Street Market

5 Chinatown Street Market

MAP K4 ■ Trengganu St & Pagoda St ■ Open 10am–11pm daily

Closed to vehicles, these two streets are lined with stalls selling a jumble of gifts and trinkets, mainly from China. There are also batiks and carved wood items, most likely from Indonesia, and lacquerware and silk items from Vietnam. Behind the stalls, stores sell pricier gifts, art, and antiques. Nearby Smith Street is closed to traffic, as food is served from roadside stalls.

6 Jamae Chulia Mosque

MAP K4 ■ 218 South Bridge Rd ■ 6221-4165 ■ Open 10:30am–6pm daily, closed 12:15–2:30pm Fri

The Chulias were Muslims who were engaged in trade and money-changing and who came from India's

Jamae Chulia Mosque minarets

southern coast. They financed the building of the nearby Al-Abrar Mosque as well as this one. The impressive facade of Jamae Chulia is southern Indian in style, with lattice-work embellishment and two tall minarets with *mihrabs* (small niches) carved in the sides. Cloaks are available inside the entrance for visitors wearing shorts or sleeveless tops.

7 Thian Hock Keng Temple

Though a main stop on every tourist itinerary, Thian Hock Keng maintains its authenticity. Built in the architectural style of southern Chinese temples, it follows *feng shui*, traditional rules that govern the placement of objects for optimal flow of energy. Though Taoist and dedicated to the goddess Ma Zu (Ma Cho Po), it respects Buddhist teachings, too, with a shrine of Bodhisattva Guanyin and the Buddhist swastika embellishing its walls (see pp16–17).

8 Ann Siang Hill Park

MAP K4, L4 ■ Park entrances: Amoy St & Club St

Chinatown and Tanjong Pagar were once covered in hills, but most have been levelled. Ann Siang Hill is one of the few that remains. This park stretches along the hilltop, with stairs and boardwalks offering views over shophouse rooftops.

9 Buddha Tooth Relic Temple

MAP K4 ▪ 288 South Bridge Rd
▪ 6220-0220 ▪ Open 7am–7pm daily
▪ www.btrts.org.sg

This complex, completed in 2007 at a cost of S$53 million, houses a sacred tooth relic of the Buddha. The building contains halls for prayer and meditation, a theater, museums, an exhibition center, a gift shop, and a teahouse. While the layout is based on the Buddhist order of the cosmos, the architecture is inspired by the Tang Dynasty of China. Shorts, skirts, and sleeveless tops are not allowed.

Icon, Buddha Tooth Relic Temple

10 Singapore City Gallery

MAP K5 ▪ 45 Maxwell Rd
▪ 6321-8321 ▪ Open 9am–5pm
Mon–Sat ▪ www.ura.gov.sg

Housed at the Urban Redevelopment Authority – Singapore's central planning agency – this gallery gives an overview of heritage conservation and future grand projects, aided by huge scale models of the island. Regular guided tours present the official view of what Singapore needs next.

ENTER THE TOURIST

In the early 1980s, the city recognized the value of preserving its architectural heritage and began restoring historic buildings. Crumbling shophouses have been restored to their original beauty, and streets once bustling with hawkers now host souvenir shops, giving Chinatown a vibrant feel.

A DAY IN CHINATOWN

Chinatown MRT
Chinatown Heritage Centre
Pagoda Street
Jamae Chulia Mosque
Chinatown Street Market
Club Street
Sri Mariamman Temple
Ann Siang Hill Park
Buddha Tooth Relic Temple
Maxwell Food Centre
Thian Hock Keng Temple

▶ MORNING

From the Chinatown MRT, take the overhead walkway across Eu Tong Sen Street and New Bridge Road to Pagoda Street. Start the day here, at the **Chinatown Heritage Centre** *(see p71)*, which will give you an overview of the neighborhood's rich history. Outside, meander past the stalls of the **Chinatown Street Market** at Pagoda and Trengganu streets, where shops sell drinks and snacks. Nearby, on South Bridge Road, is the perfect example of multicultural harmony in Singapore. Here, you can visit the **Jamae Chulia Mosque** on the corner of Mosque Street, the **Sri Mariamman Temple** *(see p71)*, and the **Buddha Tooth Relic Temple**, situated on South Bridge Road.

AFTERNOON

Have an authentic local lunch and something cool to drink at one of the foodstalls at the **Maxwell Food Centre** *(see p60)* opposite the **Buddha Tooth Relic Temple**. If you prefer to eat lunch in a restaurant, stroll up Ann Siang Hill to Club Street, where you will find a selection of chic Asian and international restaurants in restored shophouses. After lunch, take a stroll along Club Street to admire the architecture, then take the shortcut through **Ann Siang Hill Park** to Amoy Street, where many legal, public relations, and advertising firms have offices. The park ends just behind the **Thian Hock Keng Temple** *(see pp16–17)*.

See map on p70

Chinese Cultural Experiences

1 Chinatown Night Market
MAP K4 ▪ Pagoda St

Watch sidewalk calligraphers translate foreign names into Chinese characters *(see p76)*.

Chinatown Night Market calligrapher

2 Eu Yan Sang Clinic for Traditional Medicine
MAP K4 ▪ 273 South Bridge Rd ▪ 6223-6333 ▪ Open 9am–6:30pm Mon–Sat ▪ www.euyansang.com.sg

Over 45 per cent of Singaporeans use traditional Chinese medicine. The Eu Yan Sang dispensary has branches across Singapore and Malaysia.

3 Eu Yan Sang Clinic for Acupuncture
MAP K4 ▪ 273 South Bridge Rd ▪ 6223-6333 ▪ Open 9am–6:30pm Mon–Sat ▪ Adm

Head here for acupuncture – the needles stimulate positive energy in the body to treat illness and disease.

4 Chinese Theatre Circle
MAP K4 ▪ 5 Smith St ▪ 6323-4862 ▪ Open noon–5pm Tue–Sat, 2–6pm Sun ▪ www.ctcopera.com.sg ▪ Adm

There are karaoke-style Chinese opera shows in the afternoon followed by formal evening shows with meals on Fridays and Saturdays.

5 Da Wei Arts n Crafts
MAP K4 ▪ 270 South Bridge Rd ▪ 6224-5058 ▪ Open 11am–7:30pm daily

This store stocks Chinese art supplies such as paper, ink, and brushes.

6 Nanyin Music
MAP L4 ▪ Thian Hock Keng Temple, 158 Telok Ayer St ▪ www.siongleng.com

Every year, the temple hosts a handful of evening performances of traditional Chinese music in the southern nanyin style. The local Siong Leng organization runs this.

7 Nam's Supplies
MAP K4 ▪ 22 Smith St ▪ 6324-5872 ▪ Open 8am–6pm daily

This store sells fake banknotes and paper replicas of luxury goods ("hell money"), burned to reach departed souls in the afterlife.

8 Chinese Chess
MAP K4 ▪ Sago St & Trengganu St

Amid touristy shops, old locals still gather to play chess.

9 The Tea Chapter
MAP K5 ▪ 9A 11 Neil Rd ▪ 6226-1175 ▪ Open 11am–10:30pm daily (until 11pm Fri & Sat) ▪ www.teachapter.com ▪ Adm

Learn the art of the traditional Chinese tea ceremony while you relax in this teahouse.

10 Wet Market
MAP K4 ▪ Chinatown Complex ▪ Open 5am–noon Tue–Sun

The floors of this market are hosed with water daily. It sells fruit, vegetables, meats, and dried goods.

Fish stall at Chinatown's Wet Market

Restaurants

PRICE CATEGORIES

For a three-course meal for one with a non-alchoholic drink (or equivalent meal), taxes, and extra charges.
$ under S$30 $$ S$30–70 $$$ over S$70

(1) Momma Kong's
MAP K4 ▪ 34 Mosque St
▪ 6225-2722 ▪ Open 5–11pm Mon–Fri, 11am–11pm Sat & Sun ▪ $$

This compact eatery specializes in Singaporean crab classics such as chili crab and crab *bee hoon* noodle soup. Kids eat free at weekend lunchtimes.

(2) Yum Cha
MAP K4 ▪ 20 Trengganu St
▪ 6372-1717 ▪ Open 11am–11pm Mon–Fri, 9am–11pm Sat & Sun ▪ $$

A popular old-style shophouse serving delicious freshly made dim sum, Cantonese treats such as Peking duck, and crispy pastries.

(3) IndoChine @ Club Street

Silk, incense, and candles create a lounge ambience in which to enjoy delicious food from Laos, Vietnam, and Cambodia. Try the Lao-style chicken curry *(see p58)*.

(4) Da Paolo HQ
MAP K4 ▪ 80 Club St ▪ 6479-6522 ▪ Open 11:30am–2:30pm & 6:30–10:30pm Mon–Fri, 6:30–10:30pm Sat ▪ $$

The elegant Da Paolo has Italian specialties such as rack of lamb and spaghetti with squid ink. Founded in 1989, it is a Singapore classic.

(5) Lee Tong Kee
278 South Bridge Rd
▪ 6226-0417 ▪ Open 11am–4pm Mon (until 9pm Wed–Sat), 10:30am–9pm Sun ▪ $

This cheap and cheerful noodle house specializes in *hor fun* (tagliatelle-like rice noodles), mostly stir-fried with assorted accompaniments.

(6) Lucha Loco
MAP K5 ▪ 15 Duxton Hill
▪ 6226-3938 ▪ Open 5pm–12am Tue–Thu, 5pm–1am Fri, 6pm–1am Sat ▪ $$

This energetic Mexican restaurant has a great garden-bar and terrace.

(7) Blue Ginger
MAP K5 ▪ 97 Tanjong Pagar Rd
▪ 6222-3928 ▪ Open noon–2:30pm & 6:30–10:30pm daily ▪ $$

This is the best place to try Peranakan cuisine, such as *ayam buah keluak* – chicken curry with candlenuts.

Quirky interior at Potato Head Folk

(8) Potato Head Folk
MAP K4 ▪ 36 Keong Saik Rd
▪ 6327-1939 ▪ Open 11am–12am daily ▪ $$

The international menu makes nods to Asia, but really it is all about the burgers and cocktails here.

(9) Annalakshmi
MAP K4 ▪ 01–04 Central Square, 20 Havelock Rd ▪ 6339-9993 ▪ Open 11:15am–3pm & 6:15–9:30pm daily ▪ No prices; payment by donation

Enjoy Indian vegetarian buffets at this place operated by the Temple of Fine Arts, a charity for art and music.

(10) Ci Yan Organic Health Food
MAP K4 ▪ 8 Smith St ▪ 6225-9026 ▪ Open noon–10pm daily ▪ $

Sample Chinese vegetarian meals from a menu that changes daily.

See map on p70

Shopping

1 Yue Hwa Chinese Emporium
MAP K4 ▪ 70 Eu Tong Sen St ▪ 6538-4222 ▪ Open 11am–9pm daily (10pm Sat)

This emporium is recommended for its variety of Chinese handicrafts, from silk clothing to embroidered linen, jade jewelry, and gifts at affordable prices.

Chop, Chinatown Seal Carving

2 Chinatown Night Market
MAP K4 ▪ Pagoda St & Trengganu St ▪ Open 11am–11pm daily

The name is misleading, since stalls open during the day, too. Every kind of souvenir is sold, but shop around to compare prices (see p74).

Stalls in the Chinatown Night Market

3 Yong Gallery
MAP K4 ▪ 260 South Bridge Rd ▪ 6226-1718 ▪ Open 10am–7pm daily

This gallery combines two ancient arts: calligraphy and wood carving.

4 Zhen Lacquer Gallery
MAP K4 ▪ 1 Trengganu St ▪ 6222-2718 ▪ Open 10:30am–9pm daily

This small, friendly shop specializes in lacquerware products, including some attractive bowls.

5 Orchid Chopsticks
MAP K4 ▪ 42 Pagoda St ▪ 6423-0488 ▪ Open 10am–10pm daily

The ornamental and customized chopsticks sold here make wonderful small gifts for friends and family back home.

6 Chinatown Seal Carving
MAP K4 ▪ 02–06 Lucky Chinatown, 211 New Bridge Rd ▪ 9817-8781 ▪ Open 11am–8pm Mon–Sat, 11am–7pm Sun

Craftsmen here will translate your name or chosen message into Chinese characters and carve it onto your choice of stone "chops" (Chinese stamps).

7 Poh Heng
MAP K4 ▪ 01–17 People's Park Complex, 1 Park Rd ▪ 6535-0960 ▪ Open 11am– 9pm daily

Specializing in gold and jade, this venerable jeweler also has some attractive Peranakan-style brooches.

8 The Tintin Shop
MAP K4 ▪ 28 Pagoda St ▪ 8183-2210 ▪ Open 10am–9pm daily

Fans of Belgian cartoonist Hergé's famous comic-book detective will find all sorts of Tintin-related merchandise at this store.

9 Chinatown Complex
MAP K4 ▪ Sago St & Trengganu St ▪ Opening times vary

This complex sells mostly household goods, but there are some unusual finds for the bargain hunter.

10 World Arts & Crafts
MAP K4 ▪ B1–28 People's Park, 101 Upper Cross St ▪ 6532-0056 ▪ Open noon–7pm daily

With a collection from as far as China and South America, this store sells crystals set in jewelry as well as in their natural rock forms.

The Best of the Rest

1 Preserved Shophouses
MAP L4 ▪ China St

The pedestrianized streets either side of China Street contain rows of shophouses, now converted into offices and restaurants as part of the China Square and Far East Square commercial growth.

2 Bee Cheng Hiang
MAP K4 ▪ 189 New Bridge Rd ▪ 6223-7059 ▪ Open 8am–10pm daily

Specializing in *bak kwa* – slices of barbecued pork – in many flavors, Bee Cheng Hiang often has lines going around the block.

3 Speakers' Corner
MAP K3 ▪ Hong Lim Park, Upper Pickering St & New Bridge Rd ▪ Open 24 hours

This stage in a public park is the official platform for public speaking in Singapore. Speakers must not use racial or religious slurs.

4 Fuk Tak Chi Museum
MAP L4 ▪ 76 Telok Ayer St ▪ Open 10am–10pm daily

Once a small shrine serving the Cantonese and Hakka groups, Fuk Tak displays a series of artifacts collected from the local Chinese community.

5 Mei Heong Yuen Dessert
MAP K4 ▪ 65–7 Temple St ▪ 6221-1156 ▪ Open noon–9:30pm Tue–Sun

Chinese desserts are the specialty here. Try the almond, walnut, and sesame pastes or a cold dessert such as Mango Snow Ice.

6 Duxton Hill
MAP K5

This small cluster of conservation shophouses is a charming retreat

Shophouse facade, Duxton Hill

during the day, and it is then beautifully lit in the evenings, when drinkers and diners come to enjoy the eclectic restaurants and bars.

7 Tong Heng Confectionery
MAP K4 ▪ 285 South Bridge Rd ▪ 6223-3649 ▪ Open 9am–10pm daily

This patisserie serves Chinese-style egg tarts, a local version of the very popular Portuguese recipe.

Mooncake, Tai Chong Kok

8 Tai Chong Kok
MAP K4 ▪ 34 Sago St ▪ Open 9am–8pm daily (6pm Mon)

Traditionally filled with lotus seed paste, the modern mooncakes sold here come in many different flavors.

9 Chinese Weekly Entertainment Club
MAP K4 ▪ 76 Club St ▪ No public access

Built in 1891, this mansion was once a draw for socialites. Now it is a secretive private members' club.

10 Club Street
MAP K4, L4

Once home to the Chinese clan associations, this lively street has boutiques, bars, and restaurants.

See map on p70

TOP 10 Little India and Kampong Glam

In the mid-19th century, ranchers settled and raised cattle in the area that is now Little India. This trade blossomed, supported by Indian labor. The government later opened brick kilns and lime pits that also relied on Indian workers; today, stores selling goods from India lend it authenticity. Kampong Glam was allocated to the Sultan of Singapore in Raffles' 1822 town plan and attracted other Muslim residents such as Malays, Bugis (from Sulawesi), and Arabs. Bugis immigrants set up ship-building firms, and some Arab companies are still in business today. Arabic culture is evident in the cafés and stores.

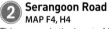
Store selling baskets on Arab Street

1 Arab Street
MAP G4, G5, H5
Named for the Arab traders who were among the earliest foreign settlers, Arab Street is the main thoroughfare in Kampong Glam, Singapore's Muslim quarter. The stores here sell batiks, baskets, fabrics, and items from Indonesia and the Middle East.

2 Serangoon Road
MAP F4, H4
This avenue is the heart of Little India, an enclave that has escaped modernization. Family-run stores still operate from old shophouses with peeling paint, and Indians still come here to buy items such as clothing, groceries, and ceremonial treasures. Inside some of the stores, spice grinders, laundrymen, and goldsmiths continue to work as they have done for decades.

LITTLE INDIA AND KAMPONG GLAM

Little India and Kampong Glam

③ Sri Srinivasa Perumal Temple

MAP G2 ■ 397 Serangoon Rd ■ 6298-5771 ■ Open 6am–noon & 6–9pm daily ■ www.sspt.org.sg

The first temple in Singapore to be built for the worship of Vishnu, Sri Srinivasa Perumal Temple has an impressive *gopuram* (main gate) with more than five tiers of figurines, including representations of Vishnu's various incarnations as well as his steed, the half-man, half-eagle Garuda. Part of the Hindu trinity, Vishnu is associated with protection, as Brahma is with creation, and Shiva with destruction. This is also the start for Thaipusam and Thimithi *(see pp66–7)*.

Sri Srinivasa Perumal Temple

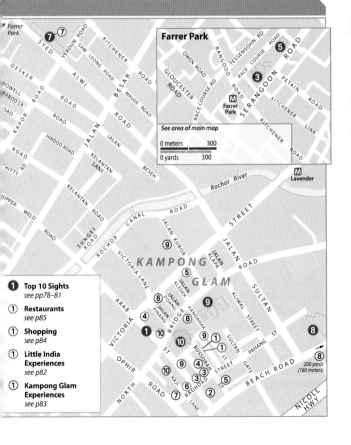

Top 10 Sights
see pp78–81

① **Restaurants**
see p85

① **Shopping**
see p84

① **Little India Experiences**
see p82

① **Kampong Glam Experiences**
see p83

Abdul Gafoor Mosque facade

4 Abdul Gafoor Mosque
MAP F4, G4 ■ **41 Dunlop Street**
■ 6295-4209 ■ Open 9:30am–9pm
(except prayer times 12:30–1:30pm
& 4:45–5:30pm) daily

This mosque is a mix of Islamic and
European architecture, with stately
columns supporting Moorish
arches. A sun motif above the
main entrance contains
names of the 25 prophets
of Islam in delicate calligraphy within its rays.

5 Malay Heritage Centre
MAP H4 ■ **85 Sultan Gate**
■ 6391-0450 ■ Compound:
8am–9pm daily; museum:
10am–6pm Tue–Sun
■ Adm (museum) ■ www.
malay heritage.org.sg

Originally Istana Kampong
Glam, the official residence of the
Sultan of Singapore, is an example
of the Neo-Classical architecture
that was popular in the early 1800s.
It is believed to have been designed
by G. D. Coleman, the Irish architect
behind many of Singapore's civic
buildings and churches, and advisor
for Raffles' town plan. In 2006, the
property was restored and reopened
as the Malay Heritage Centre.

6 Sri Veeramakaliamman Temple
Since its humble beginnings in the
mid-19th century, this temple has
been associated with the laboring
classes, as it was built mainly for
and by local workers. It was constructed for the worship of Kali, a
divine mother figure who provides
comfort to worshippers far from
home. As with all Hindu temples in
Singapore, the colorful figures on the
roof were created by skilled craftsmen brought in from southern India
especially for the job (see pp20–21).

Sri Veeramakaliamman Temple

7 Mustafa Centre
MAP G3 ■ **145 Syed
Alwi Rd** ■ 6295-5855
■ Open 24 hours ■
www.mustafa.com.sg

This enormous
department store
snakes through two
city blocks, offering
24-hour shopping for
a huge range of
Indian products.
There is everything
from ordinary, well-
discounted store goods to a stunning
collection of intricate treasures in the
gold department. The store also has
a large collection of saris, traditional
costume, jewelry, and textiles.

8 Hajjah Fatimah Mosque
MAP H5 ■ **4001 Beach Rd**
■ 6297-2774 ■ Open 10am–9pm daily

A local businesswoman, Hajjah
Fatimah, lived at this site in a house
that was repeatedly burglarized and
eventually set on fire. In gratitude for
her escape, she decided to build a
mosque here. Built around 1846,
the edifice is a mix of European,
Chinese, and Malay architecture.
Most interesting is the tilting minaret
– Singapore's take on Italy's Leaning
Tower of Pisa.

ISTANA KAMPONG GLAM

In 1824, Sultan Hussein signed away
his sovereign rights to the East India
Company in return for a plot of land.
After his death, his son Sultan Ali built
Istana Kampong Glam on the land.
Royal fortunes dwindled, and, in 1897,
a court ruled that the estate belonged to
the British crown. The royal family was
later resettled, and the state turned the
palace into the Malay Heritage Centre.

9 Sakya Muni Buddha Gaya Temple

MAP G2 ▪ 366 Race Course Rd
▪ 6294-0714 ▪ Open 8am–4:30pm daily

This small Buddhist temple is also known as the Temple of a Thousand Lights, thanks to the 989 lights that surround the main Buddha image, and are turned on for special ceremonies. Around the base of the main altar, painted murals depict episodes from the life of the Buddha. Behind the altar, a small doorway leads to an inner chamber with an image of the reclining Buddha. The temple has many Thai aesthetic influences handed down from its founder, who was a Thai monk.

10 Sultan Mosque

The most important mosque in Singapore, Sultan Mosque was built using contributions from the Muslim community. Even glass bottles donated from the poor were used for the band at the base of the onion dome. The mosque's governing body is made up of two members from each ethnic group of the local Muslim community – Malays, Javanese, Bugis, Arabs, Tamils, and North Indians (see pp18–19).

Onion dome of the Sultan Mosque

EXPLORING LITTLE INDIA AND KAMPONG GLAM

▶ MORNING

From Little India MRT station, enter the adjacent **Tekka Market** (see p84) which has lively hawker stalls and a wet market at ground level, with ethnic clothing stalls above. Then follow the main Serangoon Road north to **Sri Veeramakaliamman Temple** to witness vibrant Hindu traditions. Slightly further along is **Mustafa Centre**, a 24-hour megastore that sells literally everything in its vast and bewildering interior. Farther up Serangoon Road is **Sri Srinivasa Perumal Temple** (see p79), a peaceful place of worship. Next, take Perumal Road to Race Course Road and turn right to **Sakya Muni Buddha Gaya Temple**. Then, head through the backstreets southeast of Serangoon Road, to wander past colorful shophouses and pop into pretty **Abdul Gaffoor Mosque**.

AFTERNOON

From Little India, it is a 10-minute walk to **Kampong Glam** and lunch in one of the buzzing resto-bars of Haji Lane's (see p83). They all appeal, but a good choice is **The Singapura Club** (see p85) for comfort food. Afterwards, check out the independent boutiques along the lane and regional textiles on the adjacent Arab Street. Make a visit to the **Sultan Mosque**, at the heart of this Muslim neighborhood. From there, browse souvenirs along Bussorah Street (see p83) before heading a couple of blocks north to the **Malay Heritage Centre**.

See map on pp78–9 ←

Little India Experiences

Flower garlands for sale on Campbell Lane

(1) Flower Garlands
MAP F4 ■ Campbell Lane & Buffalo Rd

Garlands of fresh flowers are sewn together by hand and sold on street corners in this area.

(2) Anantha Ayurvedic
MAP F4 ■ Blk 661, 01–30 Buffalo Rd ■ 6396-4494 ■ Open 9am–1pm & 3–9pm Tue–Sun

Traditional Indian medicine has been practiced for more than 5,000 years. Anantha uses a range of natural, plant-based formulations for its treatments.

(3) Sajeev Studio
MAP F4 ■ 23 Kerbau Rd ■ 6296-6537 ■ Open 10:30am–10pm daily

This photographer dresses men and women in traditional Indian clothing, jewelry, and make-up for keepsake portraits.

(4) Tamil Mass
MAP G4 ■ Our Lady of Lourdes, 50 Ophir Rd ■ 6294-0624

Often busy on Sundays, Our Lady of Lourdes is one of several historic churches in the area where you can witness Christian Indian worship.

(5) The Yoga Shop
MAP F3 ■ 6 Belilios Lane ■ 6296-6566 ■ Open noon–8:30pm Mon–Fri, 10:30am–8:30pm Sat, 10:30am–5pm Sun

Sells books and other yoga-related materials, and they can also direct you to free yoga classes.

(6) ANSA Picture Framing and Art Gallery
MAP F4 ■ 29 Kerbau Rd ■ 6295-6605 ■ Open 9:30am–8:30pm Mon–Sat, 10:30am–3:30pm Sun

Browse through portraits of Hindu deities along with secular works.

(7) Spice Grinding
MAP F4 ■ 2 Cuff Rd ■ Open 9:30am–6:30pm Tue–Sun

In this shophouse, Indian spices are ground in electric mills that emit beautifully aromatic powder.

(8) Indian Heritage Centre
MAP F4 ■ 5 Campbell Lane ■ 6291-1601 ■ Open 10am–7pm Tue–Thu, until 8pm Fri & Sat, until 4pm Sun ■ Adm

Five galleries highlight the history of the local Indian community, and there's a free guided tour every day.

Indian Heritage Centre

(9) Selvi's
MAP F4 ■ 01–23, 01–11 48 Serangoon Rd & Little India Arcade ■ 6297-5322 ■ Open 9am–8:30pm daily (until 5pm Sun)

Artists apply a non-toxic paste to your hands, leaving a temporary tattoo.

(10) Betel Nuts
MAP F4 ■ Campbell Lane & Buffalo Rd

The areca seed palm is wrapped by street sellers in a leaf, to be chewed.

 See map on pp78–9

Kampong Glam Experiences

1 Malay Art Gallery
MAP H5 ▪ 31 Bussorah St
▪ 6294-8051 ▪ Open noon–8pm
Mon–Sat, 1:30–7pm Sun

Clinging on among the new Middle
Eastern restaurants, this old shop
sells examples of the *keris* – the
Malay ceremonial dagger – as well
as pricey *songket* (brocade) fabric.

2 Kampong Glam Café
MAP H5 ▪ 17 Bussorah St ▪ Open
8–3am daily ▪ Closed every other Mon

Popular with locals and tourists
alike, this roadside open-air restaurant serves Malay and Indian food.

3 Sarabat Stall
MAP H5 ▪ 21 Baghdad St
▪ Open 6:30am–11:30pm daily

This stall sells a thick mixture of
sweetened condensed milk and tea,
poured between two cups to make
it frothy. A popular local favorite.

4 Wayan Retreat Balinese Spa
MAP H5 ▪ 61 Bussorah St ▪ 6392-
0035 ▪ Open 10am–9pm Mon–Fri,
10am–8pm Sat, 10am–6pm Sun

This women's spa uses baths, wraps,
and facials to rejuvenate and relax.

5 Bussorah Street
MAP H5 ▪ Bussorah St

This wide, palm-fringed avenue
has several shops selling antiques,
curios, and souvenirs, plus Arabic
and Turkish restaurants.

6 Hjh Maimunah Restaurant
MAP G4 ▪ 11 & 15 Jalan Pisang
▪ 6297-4294 ▪ Open 7am–8pm Mon–
Sat ▪ $$

A local institution for spicy Malay
food. Go early and join the fast-
moving queue.

7 Blu Jaz Cafe
MAP H5 ▪ 11 Bali Lane ▪ 6292-
3800 ▪ Open noon–1am Mon–Thu,
noon–2am Fri, 3pm–2am Sat

This long-standing venue has a
colorful outdoor area and offers
a variety of live entertainment.

8 Golden Mile Complex
MAP H5 ▪ 5001 Beach Rd
▪ Open 10am–10pm daily

Singapore's Little Thailand attracts
residents with groceries, traditional
goods, and authentic Thai food.

9 Muslim Cemetery
MAP H4 ▪ Corner of Victoria St
& Jalan Kubor

The gravestones look haphazard, but
square stones indicate men's graves,
and round ones mark those of women.

10 Haji Lane
MAP G5, H5 ▪ 15 min walk
from Bugis MRT

A narrow back alley with offbeat
stores that sell locally designed
clothing and imported oddities.

Quaint stores on Haji Lane

Shopping

1 Ratianah
MAP H5 ▪ 23 Bussorah St
▪ 6392-0323 ▪ Open 12:30–9pm
Mon–Sat, 1–5pm Sun
Peranakan-style fabrics and
women's clothes are sold at this
Malay-run shop, plus some jewelry.

2 Sri Ganesh Textiles
MAP F4 ▪ 100 Serangoon Rd
▪ 6298-2029 ▪ Open 9:30am–9:30pm
daily
This shop has a wide assortment of
high-quality saris from India, Japan,
China, and Indonesia.

3 Rishi Handicrafts
MAP H5 ▪ 5 Baghdad St
▪ 6298-2408 ▪ Open 10am–5:30pm
daily
All sorts of baskets, woven hats,
mats, and bags, mostly from
Indonesia and China, are available
at this Baghdad Street landmark.

4 StyleMart
MAP F4 ▪ 149–151 Selegie Rd
▪ 6338-2073 ▪ Open 11am–8:45pm
Mon–Sat, noon–6:30pm Sun
A boutique specializing in fine,
formal Indian fashions, such as
embroidered and beaded silks and
brocades – perfect for gifts.

5 Little India Arcade
MAP F4 ▪ 48 Serangoon Rd
▪ Open 9am–10pm daily
A cluster of stores here sells
costume jewelry, tapestries,
Bollywood DVDs, incense, leather
goods, and Indian fashions.

Saris for sale in Tekka Market

6 Tekka Market
MAP F3 ▪ 665 Buffalo Rd
▪ Open 6am–10pm daily
This landmark building offers a wet
market, hawker stalls, and stores
stocking inexpensive Indian clothing.

7 Mustafa Centre
Although the 24-hour Mustafa
Centre sells everything under the
sun, its best offerings are Indian
imports – silk saris, gold jewelry,
and woven textiles (see p80).

8 Jamal Kazura Aromatics
MAP H4 ▪ 728 North Bridge Rd
▪ 6293-2350 ▪ Open 10am–6pm Mon–
Fri (until 2pm Sat)
This store sells oil-based fragrances
for those Muslims who may wish to
avoid contact with alcohol.

9 Basharahil Brothers
MAP H5 ▪ 101 Arab St ▪ 6296-
0432 ▪ Open 10am–6pm Mon–Sat,
11am–5pm Sun
Cotton and silk batik cloth, imported
from Indonesia, is sold here by the
meter or in the form of sarongs,
placemats, tablecloths,
and napkins.

10 Batu Pahat Goldsmith
2 Buffalo Rd ▪ 6293-1731
One of the oldest Little
India jewelers, this
shop sells gold bangles,
accessories, and
elaborate jewelry.

Little India Arcade

Restaurants

PRICE CATEGORIES

For a three-course meal for one with a non-alcoholic drink (or equivalent meal), taxes, and extra charges.

$ under S$30 $$ S$30–70 $$$ over S$70

1 Jaggi's Northern Indian Cuisine
MAP F3 ▪ 37–39 Chander Rd ▪ 6296-6141 ▪ Open 11:30am–3pm & 5:30–10:30pm Mon–Sat, 11am–10:30pm Sun ▪ $

Enjoy delicious Indian curries, plus meats and freshly baked breads from Jaggi's tandoor oven.

2 Komala Vilas
MAP F4 ▪ 76 Serangoon Rd ▪ 6293-6980 ▪ Open 11am–3:30pm & 6–10:30pm daily ▪ $

One of the quickest lunches around. The specialty, *dosai*, is a hot pancake served with gravy. Dishes are vegetarian and very good value.

3 Muthu's Curry
MAP F3 ▪ 138 Race Course Rd ▪ 6392-1722 ▪ Open 10:30am–10:30pm daily ▪ $$

Muthu's is home to Singapore's favorite fish-head curry. Various southern Indian dishes are served, too.

4 Nabins
MAP H5 ▪ 150 Arab St ▪ 6299-3267 ▪ Open 11–3am daily ▪ $

Though mostly Arabic, Nabins serves other cuisines too. Belly dancers perform occasionally.

5 Symmetry
MAP H4 ▪ 9 Jalan Kubor ▪ 6291-9901 ▪ Open 10:30am–11pm (until 9pm Mon, until midnight Fri), 9am–midnight Sat (until 7pm Sun) ▪ $$

This casual café-bar by day becomes a hipster diner at night, serving French-inspired meat-heavy cuisine with laid-back Australian hospitality. Plates are designed to be shared.

6 The Singapura Club
MAP H5 ▪ 26 Haji Lane ▪ 6438-0168 ▪ Open 10am–midnight daily ▪ $$

Food is Asian and Raj-inspired, plus there is a diverse cocktail menu.

7 The Banana Leaf Apollo
MAP F3 ▪ 56–58 Race Course Rd ▪ 6297-1595 ▪ Open 10:30am–10:30pm daily ▪ $

Named for the leaf on which south Indian cuisine is served, this spot also offers north Indian dishes.

Fish curry, The Banana Leaf Apollo

8 Gokul Vegetarian Restaurant
MAP F4 ▪ 19 Upper Dickson Rd ▪ 6396-7769 ▪ Open 10:30am–10pm daily ▪ $

Gokul offers vegetarian versions of Singapore's most famous dishes.

9 Rumah Makan Minang
MAP H4, H5 ▪ 18 & 18A Kandahar St ▪ 6294-4805 ▪ Open 7am–8pm Mon–Fri, until 5pm Sat & Sun ▪ $

This restaurant serves up a delicious beef and chicken *rendang* (curry), among other Indonesian dishes.

10 Zam Zam
MAP G5 ▪ 697–699 North Bridge Rd ▪ 6298-7011 ▪ Open 8am–11pm daily ▪ $

Zam Zam is famed for *murtabak*, an Indian bread filled with onion, meat, and egg, and dipped in curry.

See map on pp78–9

TOP 10 Colonial District

Before the arrival of Sir Thomas Stamford Raffles, Singapore was just a small fishing village surrounded by jungle. In time, the jungle gave way to building programs to house the local, and eventually colonial, government. The hill overlooking the Colonial District was cleared and a grand governor's residence built on top, complete with its own botanical gardens. In the 1800s, development increased and the district expanded rapidly; many of the existing buildings date from this era. The oldest part of Singapore is Fort Canning, a hilltop park. Here visitors will find a well-tended grave, believed to be that of Iskandar Shah, who ruled Singapore in the 14th century but moved on to found Melaka in Malaysia.

Statue of Sir Thomas Stamford Raffles

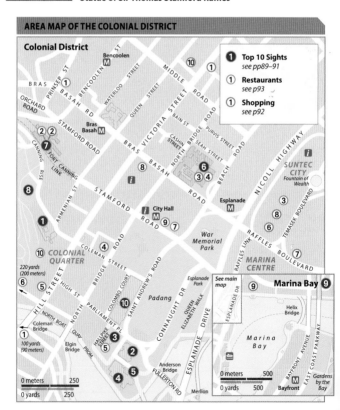

AREA MAP OF THE COLONIAL DISTRICT

Colonial District

1 Top 10 Sights	see pp89–91
1 Restaurants	see p93
1 Shopping	see p92

Previous pages Statue of Sir Stamford Raffles at Raffles' Landing Site

Stamp, Singapore Philatelic Museum

1 Singapore Philatelic Museum

MAP L2 ▪ **23B Coleman Street**
▪ **6337-3888** ▪ **Open 10am–7pm daily** ▪ **Adm** ▪ **www.spm.org.sg**

This museum documents Singapore's history and heritage through its own collection of rare stamps, as well as those on loan from private collectors. Visiting exhibits display stamp collections from around Southeast Asia.

2 Victoria Theatre and Concert Hall

MAP M3 ▪ **9 Empress Place**
▪ **6908-8810** ▪ **www.vtvch.com**

The Town Hall, completed in 1862, was the first structure purpose-built for the colonial government. The government soon outgrew the premises, and in 1909, the building was converted into a theater. The adjacent concert hall, now home to the Singapore Symphony Orchestra (SSO), was finished in 1905. Both venues were then dedicated to Queen Victoria.

Victoria Theatre and Concert Hall

3 Old Parliament House

Before Raffles' Town Plan was fully implemented (see p90), construction began on Singapore's first modern structure – a mansion for Scottish merchant John Maxwell, built in 1826 and later sold to the government. In 1999, the government moved to the new granite Parliament House next door, and the old building has been converted into The Arts House (see p42).

4 The Empress Place Building/Asian Civilisations Museum

Since Maxwell's House was too small for the growing colonial administration, a new government office was built. The oldest part was erected in 1864, with three extensions being added before it was reopened in 1905 as the Empress Place Building. It continued to be used for offices until the 1980s. Among these was the Registry of Births and Deaths – it was said that every Singaporean passed through its doors. In 2002, the building became the Asian Civilisations Museum (see pp14–15).

5 Statue of Raffles

MAP M3 ▪ **9 Empress Place**

This bronze statue of Sir Stamford Raffles was erected at the Padang in 1887, and it was moved to its current location outside the Victoria Theatre and Concert Hall in 1919, to mark Singapore's first centennial. A replica is perched at the spot along the Singapore River where it is believed that Raffles first set foot on the island in 1819.

Vast atrium of the Raffles Hotel

RAFFLES' TOWN PLAN OF 1822

In 1822, Sir Stamford Raffles formed a committee to design a plan to divide Singapore into government, residential, and commercial areas. The resulting districts still exist as the Colonial District, Chinatown, and Kampong Glam. In the Colonial District, most government buildings surrounding the Padang have been converted into museums or arts venues.

6 Raffles Hotel

The Colonial District has been the location of numerous hotels for European visitors, but only one stands today. Raffles Hotel was built from an existing bungalow in 1887, and, after extensions and renovations, has grown into an iconic landmark. W. Somerset Maugham, who was a frequent guest, famously said that the hotel stood for "all the fables of the exotic East" *(see pp30–31)*.

7 National Museum of Singapore

The National Museum has over 198,056 sq ft (18,400 sq m) of exhibit space, with galleries dedicated to presenting Singapore's history and heritage through entertaining multimedia displays. This is a highly recommended introduction to Singapore *(see pp12–13)*.

8 Fort Canning Park

MAP K1–2, L1–2 ■ Canning Rise ■ Open 24 hours daily ■ www.nparks.gov.sg

Raffles built his home at this site, but it was replaced by Fort Canning in 1860. The military stronghold atop the park's hill was impressive, but it proved useless protection, as its cannons could not reach as far as the harbor. The fort was demolished in 1929, but a Gothic gate remains. Military offices now house art groups, and the lawns host concerts. The underground

Cupolas at Fort Canning Park

bunkers, known as the Battle Box, are now an interesting World War II exhibit *(see pp44–5)*.

9 Marina Bay

Created over decades by reclaiming land, Marina Bay effectively extends the Colonial District, the financial district, and Kampong Glam southwards and eastwards. The Singapore River now flows into the "bay" – really a freshwater reservoir – with the sea kept out by the Marina Barrage. Surrounding the bay are some top-dollar attractions, notably the Marina Bay Sands hotel and casino, Esplanade, and Gardens by the Bay *(see p28–9)*.

National Gallery Singapore

10 City Hall and the Supreme Court

MAP M2 ■ St. Andrew's Rd

Completed in 1929, the City Hall was the site of many historical events. In 1945, the Japanese surrendered here; in 1959, Prime Minister Lee Kuan Yew proclaimed Singapore's self-rule on the steps; and in 1966, it was the site of Singapore's first National Day celebrations. The Supreme Court was built in 1932, and, although both buildings are massive, the government outgrew them. The judiciary now operates from the new Supreme Court building behind the original, while the City Hall offices now occupy other modern buildings. The old buildings now house the National Gallery *(see p38)*.

A WALK AROUND THE COLONIAL DISTRICT

▶ MORNING

Begin at the **National Museum** *(see pp12–13)*, where you can spend a couple of hours exploring the history of Singapore. Exit through the rear to walk through **Fort Canning Park** to soak up its heritage and amazing views. Walk down from the park onto Hill Street, and turn left to admire the 1835 **Armenian Church** *(see p40)*, Singapore's oldest church. Behind the church stands the **Peranakan Museum** *(see p38)*, which illuminates the culture of the Straits Chinese. Next, walk one block up Victoria Street to beautiful **CHIJMES** *(see p43)*, a 19th-century missionary school, which is now a shopping and dining complex.

AFTERNOON

Next to CHIJMES on Bras Basah Road is Raffles City mall, which has a good mix of premier and mainstream labels. After a shopping fix, cross Bras Basah to tour iconic **Raffles Hotel** and maybe have a Singapore Sling in the Long Bar. Exit from Raffles' main entrance on Beach Road, turn right and continue on to **St. Andrew's Cathedral** *(see p43)*. After exploring the church's nostalgic interior, follow the road south with the historic **Padang** *(see p45)* to your left and the **National Gallery Singapore** *(see p38)* to your right. Spend the rest of the afternoon at the gallery or, depending on your interests, head past the **Victoria Theatre** *(see p89)* to explore the **Asian Civilisations Museum** *(see p89)*.

See map on p88 ←

Shopping

1 Bugis Street Market
MAP G5 ▪ Bugis St ▪ Open 2–11pm daily (some stalls open 10am)

This market is packed with stalls selling all kinds of souvenirs.

2 Museum Label
MAP L1 ▪ National Museum, 93 Stamford Rd ▪ 6336-6387 ▪ Open 10am–6pm daily

The National Museum's gift shop stocks souvenirs, clothes, and trinkets with a genuinely Singaporean touch, featuring nostalgic references or glimpses of local humor.

3 Raffles Gift Shop
MAP M1 ▪ Raffles Hotel, 1 Beach Rd ▪ 6337-1886 ▪ Open 8:30am–9pm daily

Find every kind of gift, from T-shirts to bone china sets, bearing the Raffles Hotel emblem.

4 Cathay Photo
MAP L2 ▪ Peninsula Plaza, 111 North Bridge Rd ▪ 6337-4274 ▪ Open 10am–7pm Mon–Sat

This camera store offers quality stock at decent prices.

5 Artrium@MICA
Private galleries specializing in contemporary Asian art surround the atrium lobby of this government building (see p54).

6 RISIS
MAP M1 ▪ #01–367 Suntec City Tower 1, 3 Temasek Blvd ▪ 6338-8250 ▪ Open 11am–9pm daily

In 1976, a Singapore government agency found a way to preserve an orchid in 24-carat gold. Now, RISIS sells jewelry made from the national orchid, the Vanda Miss Joaquim, and other varieties.

Gold orchid, RISIS

7 The Planet Traveller
MAP N3 ▪ #03–126 Marina Square ▪ 6337-0291 ▪ Open 10:30am–9:30pm daily

The shop for travel gear, books, maps, and even luggage repair.

8 Royal Selangor
MAP M1 ▪ #01–370 Suntec City Mall, 3 Temasek Boulevard ▪ 6822-1559

Established in 1885, Royal Selangor makes tankards, home accessories, and other pewter products, which are sold worldwide.

9 Arch
MAP M3 ▪ #02–07 Esplanade Mall, 1 Esplanade Drive ▪ 6338-0161 ▪ Open 11am–9pm daily

This place sells attractive souvenirs, such as images of iconic Singapore buildings and shophouses intricately cut into wooden veneers.

10 Bugis Junction and Bugis+
MAP G5 ▪ 200–1 Victoria St ▪ Open 10am–10pm daily

These two malls linked by a bridge are hot for high-street brands. Both have a good selection of food and beverage outlets, too.

Bugis Junction and Bugis+

Restaurants

PRICE CATEGORIES
For a three-course meal for one with a
non-alchoholic drink (or equivalent meal),
taxes, and extra charges.

$ under S$30 $$ S$30–70 $$$ over S$70

1 Rendezvous Restaurant
MAP K2 ▪ 02–72 Clarke Quay,
The Central ▪ 6339-7508 ▪ Open
11am–9pm daily ▪ $

Open since the 1950s, the history of
this place is evident in its old-world
decor. The cuisine is authentic *nasi
padang*, rice-based Indonesian food.

2 Flutes
MAP L1 ▪ National Museum,
93 Stamford Rd ▪ 6338-8770 ▪ Open
11:30am–2pm & 6:30–10pm Mon–Fri,
10:30am–2:30pm & 6:30–10:30pm
Sat, 11:30am–4pm Sun ▪ $$

Serving modern European food, this
elegant restaurant also offers English
roast beef lunches on Sundays.

3 Soup Restaurant
MAP M1 ▪ B1–122 Suntec City,
3 Temasek Blvd ▪ 6333-9886 ▪ Open
11:30am–2:30pm & 5:30–10pm Mon–
Fri, 11:30am–10pm Sat & Sun ▪ $

Come here to try dishes cooked by
the Chinese women who once worked
on Singapore's construction sites,
most famously their ginger chicken.

4 Tiffin Room
MAP M1 ▪ 1 Beach Rd ▪ 6331-
1612 ▪ Open 6:30–10:30am, noon–
2pm, 3–5:30pm, & 7–10pm daily ▪ $$$

This Asian restaurant at the Raffles
Hotel is named for the Indian light
midday meal. It offers high tea and a
curry buffet lunch and dinner.

5 Timbre@The Arts House
MAP N3 ▪ 1 Old Parliament
Lane ▪ 6338-3386 ▪ Open 6–1am
Mon–Thu, until 2am Fri & Sat ▪ $$

Located on the river, this is a great
spot to catch a live local band as you
dine. The menu is broad and western,
featuring pizzas, tapas, and steaks.

6 Quayside Seafood
MAP K2 ▪ 3A River Valley Rd,
Clarke Quay ▪ 6338-3195 ▪ Open 4pm–
midnight daily (until 1am Fri & Sat ▪ $$

This alfresco, riverfront eatery
serves fresh local-style seafood.

7 Prego
MAP M1 ▪ Fairmont Hotel,
80 Bras Basah Rd ▪ 6431-6156 ▪ Open
6–11am, 11:30am–2:30pm, 5–10:30pm
daily (from noon–3pm Sun) ▪ $$

Enjoy a range of excellent thin-crust
pizzas at this Italian restaurant.

8 Lei Garden
MAP M1 ▪ #01–24 CHIJMES,
30 Victoria St ▪ 6339-3822 ▪ Open
11:30am–2:30pm & 6–11pm daily ▪ $$

Authentic Cantonese cuisine within the
historic CHIJMES complex *(see p43)*.

Dining room of Equinox

9 Equinox
MAP M2 ▪ Swissôtel,
2 Stamford Rd ▪ 6837-3322
▪ Open noon–2:30pm (until 3pm
Sun) & 5–10:30pm daily ▪ $$$

Great views and fine dining in one
of Southeast Asia's tallest hotels.

10 Lewin Terrace
MAP L1 ▪ 21 Lewin Terrace
▪ 6333-9905 ▪ Open noon–3pm &
6:30–11pm daily ▪ $$$

This romantic restaurant serves
upscale Japanese-French-fusion
cuisine. It has a menu of fine wines.

See map on p88

TOP 10 Orchard Road

Orchard Road gets its name from the plantations that were developed here in the 1830s to grow fruit, nutmeg, pepper, and other spices. By the mid-1800s, the plantations had been wiped out by disease and the European population had grown, demanding more space. Orchard Road cut through a narrow valley and was subject to flooding, but once drainage plans were in place, businesses settled in the area to serve the colonial expatriate community.

The Istana

① The Istana and Sri Temasek

The Istana was considered expensive for a governor's residence, but, upon the building's completion in 1869, its design won critics over. Situated at the top of a hill, it is surrounded by tropical gardens. Sri Temasek, a smaller building in the compound, was built for colonial officers *(see p43)*.

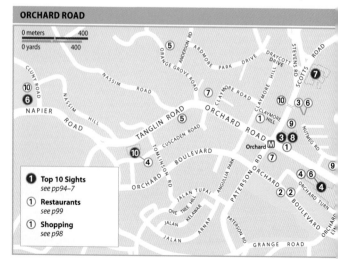

ORCHARD ROAD

0 meters 400
0 yards 400

① **Top 10 Sights**
see pp94–7

① **Restaurants**
see p99

① **Shopping**
see p98

Colorful houses on Emerald Hill Road

2 Emerald Hill Road
MAP C4–5

Away from Orchard Road, Emerald Hill Road is surprisingly tranquil. A lane of millionaires' homes, the Hill's Peranakan-style row houses have been well restored. There are several house styles, from plain, boxy 19th-century buildings to the pre-war Chinese Baroque-style terrace houses, and even ornate Art Deco variations of the 1950s shophouse.

3 Tangs
MAP B4 ▪ 310 Orchard Rd ▪ 6737-5500 ▪ Open 10:30am–9:30pm Mon–Sat, 11am–8:30pm Sun ▪ www.tangs.com

This homegrown department store sprouted from the dreams of a door-to-door salesman who arrived from China in 1923. Called the "Tin Trunk Man," C. K. Tang carried goods in a tin trunk that became his trademark. Tang bought this prime piece of property in 1958 to be near the European settlements in the area. His family still owns the department store and the plot of land on which it sits, located at a busy crossroad. Tangs has two stores in Singapore: Orchard Road and VivoCity (see p62).

4 Ngee Ann City
MAP B4, B5, C4, C5 ▪ 391 Orchard Rd ▪ Open 10am–9:30pm daily ▪ www.ngeeanncity.com.sg

Owned by the Ngee Ann Kongsi, a clan association, this spectacular shopping mall is designed like a city-within-a-city. Its oriental facade complements the western interior to create a unique cosmopolitan ambience, and it makes a majestic statement along Orchard Road. Its largest tenant is Takashimaya, a retail giant in Japan. The mall houses more than 30 restaurants, while book lovers can browse the selection at the expansive Kinokuniya bookstore.

Entrance to Ngee Ann City mall

Street performer on Orchard Road

5 Street Performances
MAP A4–C4, C5–E5
▪ Orchard Rd

Singapore liberalized public performance regulations in 2000, paving the way for street musicians, comedians, and magicians. Various international busker festivals invite some of the world's best street performers to work the crowds. The sidewalks on Orchard Road have been widened to accommodate special performance areas for buskers. The tourism board (see p112) provides information about planned busker events.

6 Singapore Botanic Gardens

These lovely gardens show visitors the area's agricultural origins, and remind residents that the city was once covered in lush tropical forest. The gardens are a favorite spot for joggers in the mornings, for photographers in the late afternoons, and, on the weekends, for families, who come for the Jacob Ballas Children's Garden. There are also music performances, and movie screenings by the lakes (see pp24–5).

Orchid, Singapore Botanic Gardens

7 Goodwood Park Hotel
MAP B3 ▪ 22 Scotts Rd ▪ 6737-7411 ▪ www.goodwoodparkhotel.com

Built in 1900, this hotel began as the Teutonia Club, an enclave for expatriate Germans. In 1929, it was converted into Goodwood Park Hotel, for businessmen from Malaya. It has withstood both World Wars, and much of the original beauty – fluted columns, delicate woodwork, decorative plasterwork, and graceful archways – has been faithfully restored. There are several award-winning restaurants, too.

THE STAMFORD CANAL

Orchard Road's malls sit above a huge canal that drains storm water, protecting the entire area from flash floods during frequent monsoon downpours. The Stamford Canal begins at Tanglin Road, runs beneath Wisma Atria and Ngee Ann City, and continues past City Hall and into Marina Bay.

Goodwood Park Hotel

8 Crossroads Café

MAP B4 ■ Singapore Marriott Hotel, 320 Orchard Rd ■ 6831-4605 ■ 7am–1am daily ■ www.singapore marriott.com

One of Singapore's best spots for people-watching, this alfresco café sits at the city's busiest intersection between Orchard, Scotts, and Paterson roads. The sidewalks teem with hordes of bustling shoppers. Virtually every tourist passes this spot, as do locals who come to Orchard Road for the malls, teenagers who flock here to hang out, and, on weekends, foreign maids who gather to catch up with friends.

Skateboarding at Skate Park

9 Skate Park and *SCAPE

MAP C5 ■ 2 Orchard Link ■ www.scape.sg

The skate park hums into the night, while the adjacent *SCAPE creative space attracts the city's youth with free gigs, dance events, and festivals. Young locals also congregate at the neighboring Cathay Cineleisure for movie screenings and to browse the stalls at *SCAPE marketplace.

10 Tanglin Mall

MAP A4 ■ Tanglin Rd

Known as an expat enclave, Tanglin Mall is a popular place for expatriates to shop for imported groceries and special goods. The US, UK, and Australian embassies and the British Council are across the street.

A STROLL ALONG ORCHARD ROAD

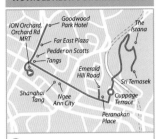

▶ MORNING

Start at Orchard Road MRT station, which will plunge you straight into multilevel **ION Orchard** (see p63) for designer and mainstream shopping. Be sure to visit ION Sky on the 56th floor for 360-degree city views, before crossing Orchard Road to iconic **Tangs** department store (see p95). From Tangs, swing down Scotts Road to **Far East Plaza** (see p62), **Pedder on Scotts** (see p98) and colonial **Goodwood Park Hotel**. Back on Orchard, the next mall stop is **Ngee Ann City** (see p95), where you can browse in the city's largest bookstore, Kinokuniya Singapore, or visit **Shanghai Tang** for contemporary Chinese-inspired design (see p98). Continue down Orchard Road to the junction at Peranakan Place on your left. This nook has good cafés for people-watching.

AFTERNOON

From Peranakan Place, enter **Emerald Hill Road** (see p95) to view enviable private homes converted from Peranakan shophouses (No. 5 retains many original details). Walk back to Orchard Road, where detours into the many malls can occupy the rest of the afternoon. You can refresh yourself with a drink at nearby **Cuppage Terrace**, popular with expats and tourists, or try a local dessert at a food court (there's one in every mall). On selected public holidays, you can visit **the Istana and Sri Temasek** (see p94), located past the intersection with Clemenceau Avenue.

See map on pp94–5

Shopping

Asian-inspired clothing and homewares for sale at Shanghai Tang

1 Tangs
This enduring, home-grown department store offers a broad range of fashion (see p95).

2 Takashimaya
MAP B4 ■ 391 Orchard Rd ■ 6738-1111 ■ Open 10am–9:30pm daily

One of Japan's oldest retailers, this huge store stocks apparel, cosmetics, and household items.

3 Paragon
One of the several Orchard Road malls, Paragon makes a play for high-end custom and is home to Armani, Calvin Klein, and Gucci, among other big names (see p63).

4 Kinokuniya Singapore
MAP B4 ■ #04–20 Ngee Ann City, 391 Orchard Rd ■ 6737-5021 ■ Open 10am–9:30pm Sun–Fri, 10am–10pm Sat

This quality bookstore has an excellent selection of fiction and non-fiction, plus magazines, including some foreign-language titles.

5 Naga Arts & Antiques
MAP A4 ■ #01–48 Tanglin Shopping Centre, 19 Tanglin Rd ■ 6235-7084 ■ Open 10:30am–6pm Mon–Sat

With furniture from Tibet, Buddha images from Burma, and textiles from China, Naga promises a terrific opportunity for bargain-hunters.

6 Shanghai Tang
MAP B4 ■ #03–06 Ngee Ann City ■ 6737-3537 ■ Open 10am–9:30pm daily

A luxury brand featuring clothing inspired by China's fashion heritage, with a modern twist. Homewares and gifts, too.

7 Charles & Keith
MAP C5 ■ #02–46, 313 Somerset Rd ■ 6509-5040 ■ Open 10:30am–10pm daily (until 10:30pm Fri & Sat)

This Singapore fashion and accessories brand specializes in women's shoes, bags, and belts.

8 CYC The Custom Shop
MAP A4 ■ #03–16A Orchard Gateway, 277 Orchard Rd ■ 6737-5332 ■ Open 11am–8:30pm daily

The attention to detail makes CYC one of the city's finest shirt makers.

9 Pedder on Scotts
MAP B4 ■ Scotts Sq, 6 Scotts Rd ■ 6244-2883 ■ Open 10am–9pm daily

A futuristic store of over 100 brands of fashion footwear and accessories, from sports shoes to Louboutin.

10 T Galleria by DFS
MAP B4 ■ 25 Scotts Rd ■ 6229-8100 ■ Open 11am– 8pm Sun–Thu, until 9pm Fri & Sat

The world's largest duty-free luxury-goods retailer delivers purchases to the airport to pick up on departure.

Restaurants

1 Les Amis
MAP B4 ■ #01–16 Shaw Centre, 1 Scotts Rd ■ 6733-2225 ■ Open noon–2:30pm & 7–10pm daily (from 6:30 Fri & Sat) ■ $$$

The contemporary French menu here has won countless awards.

2 Crystal Jade Palace
MAP B4 ■ #04–19 391 Orchard Rd ■ 6735-2388 ■ Open 11:30am–3pm, 6–11pm daily ■ $$

The flagship restaurant of the Crystal Jade chain serves Cantonese dishes.

3 mezza9
MAP B4 ■ Grand Hyatt, 10 Scotts Rd ■ 6416-7189 ■ Open 6–10:30pm daily, noon–3pm Mon–Sat, 11:30am–3pm Sun ■ $$$

This modern restaurant offers both Asian and Western cuisine, and has its own patisserie and martini bar.

4 Patara Fine Thai
03–14 Tanglin Mall ■ 6737-0818 ■ Open noon–3pm & 6–10pm daily ■ $$

Authentic Thai food is complemented by interesting Western flavors.

"Crustacean Station" at The Line

5 The Line
MAP A3 ■ Shangri-La Hotel, 22 Orange Grove Rd ■ 6213-4275 ■ Open 6–10:30am, noon–2:30pm, & 6–10pm Mon–Fri, 6–11am, noon–3pm, & 6–10:30pm Sat & Sun ■ $$$

A vast buffet of 16 food stations serves tandoori, sushi, meats, salads, stir fries, and pasta.

6 StraitsKitchen
MAP B4 ■ Grand Hyatt, 10 Scotts Rd ■ 6732-1234 ■ Open 6:30–10:30am & noon–2:30pm Mon–Fri, 6:30–11am & 12:30–3pm Sat & Sun, and 6:30–11:30pm daily ■ $$

The best of local cuisine, with excellent buffet lunches and dinners.

7 Hua Ting Restaurant
MAP A3, A4 ■ Orchard Hotel, 442 Orchard Rd ■ 6739-6666 ■ Open 11:30am–2:30pm & 6–10pm daily (from 11am Sat & Sun) ■ $$

This is the place to visit for a wide range of delicious dim sum and fine authentic Cantonese dishes.

8 Tandoor North Indian Restaurant
MAP D5 ■ Holiday Inn Parkview, 11 Cavenagh Rd ■ 6733-8333 ■ Open noon–2:30pm & 7–10:30pm daily ■ $$

An award-winning place serving Singapore's best north Indian food.

9 Tambuah Mas
MAP A4 ■ #04–10 Tanglin Shopping Centre, 19 Tanglin Rd ■ 6733-3333 ■ Open 11am–10pm daily ■ $$

Serving up proper Indonesian home-style cooking for nearly 30 years, they also have a newer branch in Paragon shopping mall (see p63).

10 Halia at Singapore Botanic Gardens
MAP S2 ■ 1 Cluny Rd ■ 8444-1148 ■ Open noon–9:30pm Sun–Thu, until 10pm Fri, 10am–10pm Sat ■ $$

In lush foliage near the Ginger Garden (halia is Malay for "ginger"), this contemporary restaurant serves mainly Western food with an Asian fusion touch.

See map on pp94–5

🔟 **Farther Afield**

Singapore is only 278 sq miles (719 sq km) in size with 120 miles (193 km) of shoreline. The urban center sits at the southernmost tip of the island. At the city's outskirts, pre-war neighborhoods consist of low-rise streets with stores where traditional trades are still practiced. Beyond these, New Towns – clusters of high-rise apartment buildings – are supported by schools, businesses, and other facilities. Most new towns enjoy fast links with the city via Mass Rapid Transit trains, operating on several lines.

Henderson Waves bridge

① The Southern Ridges
MAP S3 ▪ Henderson Rd
▪ Open 24 hours daily ▪ www.nparks.gov.sg

Four parks along the coast – Mount Faber Park, Telok Blangah Hill Park, Kent Ridge Park, and West Coast Park – are connected by a series of bridges, notably the dramatic Henderson Waves. They offer some good views of Sentosa, Keppel Harbour, and the western city center.

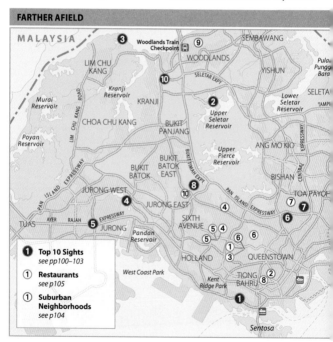

FARTHER AFIELD

Map legend:
- **①** Top 10 Sights *see pp100–103*
- **①** Restaurants *see p105*
- **①** Suburban Neighborhoods *see p104*

Singapore Zoo and Night Safari

2 Singapore Zoo, Night Safari, and River Safari

Three zoos are nestled side by side in northern Singapore. The oldest, Singapore Zoo, has guided tours, scheduled feeding times, and animal shows. The Night Safari is a novel way to see nocturnal animals at their most active. The latest addition of the trio is the River Safari, which celebrates the wildlife of the world's great rivers (see pp26-7).

3 Sungei Buloh Wetland Reserve

MAP R1 ▪ 301 Neo Tiew Crescent ▪ 6794-1401 ▪ Open 7:30am–7pm Mon–Sat, 7am–7pm Sun ▪ Adm (Sat & Sun) ▪ www.sbwr.org.sg

A series of paths and walkways leads visitors through mangrove swamps, mudflats, and pools, past an abundance of wildlife. The visitors' center shows a film featuring information on the park's history.

4 Chinese and Japanese Gardens

MAP R2 ▪ 1 Chinese Garden Rd ▪ Open 5:30am–11pm daily (Chinese Garden), 5:30am–7pm daily (Japanese Garden)

Designed to resemble an imperial garden, the arched bridges, moon gates, and twin pagodas of the Chinese Garden blend with bamboo groves, trees, and flowering shrubs. A Suzhou-style courtyard provides a serene backdrop for the garden's collection of bonsai. The adjoining Japanese Garden has a minimalist Zen feel, with pebble paths and landscaping to evoke contemplation.

5 Jurong Bird Park

MAP R2 ▪ 2 Jurong Hill ▪ 6265-0022 ▪ Open 8:30am–6pm daily ▪ Adm ▪ www.birdpark.com.sg

Visitors can easily spend half a day exploring the world's largest walk-in aviary and tons of other attractions at Jurong, including the huge collection of bird species that are native to Southeast Asia. Feeding times and bird shows are scheduled throughout the day, including lunch with parrots, where the birds show off their intelligence and dexterity.

Jurong Bird Park

Sun Yat Sen Nanyang Memorial Hall, with a statue of Sun Yat Sen in front

6 Sun Yat Sen Nanyang Memorial Hall

MAP T2 ▪ 12 Tai Gin Rd ▪ 6256-7377
▪ Open 10am–5pm Tue–Sun ▪ Adm
▪ www.sysnmh.org.sg

This grand 19th-century bungalow was a private residence before it was donated by a local businessman to Chinese revolutionary Dr. Sun Yat Sen for use as the head-quarters of his operations in Southeast Asia. In 1911, after Dr. Sun's Kuomintang Party deposed China's Qing dynasty, it was entrusted to the local Chinese Chamber of Commerce. The bungalow is now a heritage property under the National Heritage Board. The memorial hall traces Dr. Sun's revolutionary activities and highlights the impact of the 1911 Chinese Revolution on Singapore. It also documents the city's contribution to the Revolution.

Detail, Lian Shan Shuang Lin Temple

7 Lian Shan Shuang Lin Temple

MAP T2 ▪ 184 Jalan Toa Payoh
▪ 6259-6924 ▪ Open 7am–5pm daily

Singapore's oldest Buddhist monastery, whose name means "Twin Grove of the Lotus Mountain Temple," claims a 110-year history. It has three main halls – the Hall of Celestial Kings, the Mahavira Hall, and the Dharma Hall, each one built in the typical architectural style of China's southern Fujian province. The compound contains a soaring seven-story granite pagoda.

8 Bukit Timah Nature Reserve

MAP S2 ▪ 177 Hindhede Drive
▪ www.nparks.gov.sg

A rare chance to experience primary rain forest within a city, this large nature reserve has four hiking trails, taking up to two hours to complete. The park is home to a variety of birds, insects, and small mammals. It adheres to conservation acts to protect its biodiversity and prohibits

---

THE GARDEN CITY

Over 40 years ago, the then Prime Minister Lee Kuan Yew recognized the value of nature. By the 1970s, several areas had been planted with shady *angsana* trees and bougainvilleas. Since then, new urban plans have continued to be drawn up with nature in mind. The National Parks Board now manages some 23,475 acres (9,500 ha) in more than 300 parks across the city.

activities that may disturb the flora and fauna, such as feeding the long-tailed macaques. The visitors' center provides useful information to help guests navigate their way, as well as restrooms, and a first-aid station.

⑨ Pulau Ubin
MAP V1 ■ Ferries run dawn to dusk daily; take your passport ■ www.nparks.gov.sg

This island lies off Singapore's northeast coast, reached by a ferry ride from Changi Point. Rental bikes are available from the village, where there are also some restaurants. The peaceful tracks are best explored by bike, and there is also a mountain biking trail. Chek Jawa Wetlands has a boardwalk, from which you can spot marine life at low tide.

Jejawi Observation Tower, Pulau Ubin

⑩ Kranji War Memorial and Cemetery
MAP R1 ■ 9 Woodlands Rd ■ Open 7am–6pm daily

This serene cemetery, overlooking the Strait of Johor, is lined by 4,000 tombstones that mark the graves of the Australians, British, Canadians, Indians, and Malays who lost their lives during World War II. A memorial is dedicated to soldiers whose remains were never recovered.

A DAY TRIP FROM THE CITY

▶ **MORNING**

Take a Singapore Attractions Express bus (www.saeb.com.sg) direct to **Singapore Zoo** (see p101). There are two lines, each making three pick-ups per day from designated stops in the city center. Catch a 9am bus to take advantage of the cooler morning hours to tour the zoo while the animals are more active. To join the Jungle Breakfast with the orangutans, you'll need to get a taxi to reach the zoo by 9am. There are other (free) shows at set times throughout the day, 11 zones to discover, and Rainforest Kidzworld. Exploring the zoo can be tiring, but there's a hop-on hop-off tram ride, and places to get meals and snacks.

AFTERNOON

Be sure to visit the River Safari to see the giant pandas and the awe-inspiring Amazon Flooded Forest, and enjoy a boat cruise. It would be easy to spend an entire day at the zoo, but with what is left of the afternoon, head to the **Southern Ridges** (see p100). You can take a bus to the MRT from the zoo's entrance, or hop in a taxi. A good starting point for the Ridges is HarbourFront, at the end of the MRT's Circle Line. Pick up some refreshments in **VivoCity mall** (see p62) before walking up Marang Trail for spectacular views from Mount Faber. Continue west to cross the Henderson Waves bridge, which is especially atmospheric as darkness sets in.

See map on pp100–101 ⟵

Suburban Neighborhoods

1 Geylang
MAP T2

While Kampong Glam is the heart of the city's Muslim area, Geylang is Malay-influenced. The stores and eateries target locals rather than tourists, so it has a truly Malay feel.

2 Tiong Bahru
MAP S3

One of Singapore's oldest New Towns, Tiong Bahru has preserved its Art Deco buildings. It is also turning into a hub for creative artists, offering a blend of old and new. The hawker center is a must-see.

3 Katong/Joo Chiat
MAP T2

A melting-pot of Peranakan, Malay, Eurasian, Indian, and Chinese cultures, these two areas promise a treasure trove of places to eat.

Traditional houses in Katong

4 Bukit Timah
MAP S2

This sprawling suburb has several nature trails, including the hike up Singapore's highest hill. Diverse dining can be found on Sixth and Greenwood avenues.

5 Holland Village
MAP S3

Singapore's original expatriate enclave has some interesting Asian art, besides stores selling gifts and home furnishings. With trendy sidewalk cafés and bars, too, it appeals to residents of various nationalities who rub shoulders here every day.

6 Dempsey Road
MAP S2

A cluster of former military barracks set close to the Botanic Gardens, Dempsey Hill offers one-stop shopping for art, antiques, carpets, and home decor. The area's cafés, bars, and restaurants are popular on weekends and evenings.

7 Toa Payoh
MAP T2

A prime example of a New Town, Toa Payoh is centrally located and packed with high-rise apartments, with a busy mall that serves the local community. Many of the stores have been here for decades.

8 Changi Point
MAP V1

This rural seaside village has an open-air hawker center, golf course, a good beach for watersports, and a ferry terminal where you can pick up boats to Ubin island.

9 Woodlands
MAP S1

Singapore's last town before reaching Malaysia, Woodlands has a surprisingly large shopping mall, alongside a big American community that has settled here to be close to the Singapore American School.

10 Pasir Ris
MAP U2

A modern New Town, Pasir Ris is located by the sea, with beaches, watersports, waterfront parks, family activities, and alfresco hawker centers and restaurants.

Restaurants

① Au Petit Salut
MAP S3 ■ 40C Harding Rd ■ 6475-1976 ■ Open 11:30am–2:30pm & 6:30pm–11pm Tue–Sat, 10:30am–3pm Sun ■ $$$

Inside an elegant villa in leafy Dempsey Hill, this award-winning French restaurant is also renowned for its Sunday brunch.

② Long Phung Vietnamese
MAP T3 ■ 159 Joo Chiat Rd ■ 9105-8519 ■ Open 1pm–2am daily ■ $

A simple authentic eatery in lively Joo Chiat that stays crowded late into the night. Pho noodle soup is their specialty, but all dishes are generous and usually super spicy.

③ Samy's Curry Restaurant
MAP S3 ■ 25 Dempsey Rd ■ 6472-2080 ■ Open 11am–3pm & 6–10pm Wed–Mon & public hols ■ $

Visit this Indian restaurant, occupying an open-air hall amid trees, for its signature chicken masala.

④ Original Sin
MAP S3 ■ #01–62, 43 Jalan Merah Saga, Holland Village ■ 6475-5605 ■ Open 11:30am–2:30pm & 6–10:30pm daily ■ $$

Here you can enjoy Mediterranean vegetarian food enhanced with fresh ingredients and herbs, all complemented by fine wines.

⑤ Café Siem Reap
MAP S3 ■ 44 Lorong Mambong ■ 6468-5798 ■ Open 3pm–1am Sun–Thu, until 2am Fri & Sat ■ $$

A chic café adorned with replicas of Cambodian temple friezes and Buddha images. It features cuisine from Vietnam, Laos, and Cambodia.

⑥ Grand Shanghai
MAP T3 ■ 390 Havelock Rd ■ 6836-6866 ■ Open noon–2:30pm Tue–Fri & Sun, 6:30–10:30pm Tue–Sun ■ $$

Shanghainese classics are served in a 1920s ambience. The crispy eels and dim sum are favorites.

Interior of Open Door Policy

⑦ Long Beach Seafood
MAP U3 ■ 1202 East Coast Parkway ■ 6448-3636 ■ Open 11am–midnight daily ■ $$

Famed for its Sri Lankan crabs in black pepper sauce, Long Beach also serves great meat dishes.

⑧ Open Door Policy
MAP S3 ■ 19 Yong Siak St, Tiong Bahru ■ 6221-9307 ■ Open noon–3pm & 6–10pm daily ■ $$$

ODP delivers gluten- and dairy-free contemporary European fare in rustic-cool surroundings. The lunch menu is great value.

⑨ Chilli Padi Nonya Restaurant
MAP T2 ■ 11 Joo Chiat Place ■ 6275-1002 ■ Open 11:30am–2:30pm & 5:30–10pm daily ■ $

This award-winning eatery offers a selection of Peranakan favorites – unique Straits Chinese cuisine.

⑩ Al Azhar
MAP S2 ■ 11 Cheong Chin Nam Rd, Bukit Timah ■ 6466-5052 ■ Open 24 hours ■ $

Focusing on international Muslim cuisine, this bustling eatery has a huge menu, but no alcohol.

See map on pp100–101 ←

Streetsmart

**Traditional Peranakan
shophouse in Chinatown**

Getting To and Around Singapore

Arriving by Air

Changi Airport is a main hub, and more than 100 airlines operate in and out of Singapore. There are frequent direct flights to major cities including London, New York, Paris, and Sydney. Several low-cost carriers such as **Tigerair**, **JetStar**, and **Air Asia** offer budget flights across the region.

Free English-language city tours are available for stopover passengers with a wait of more than 5.5 hours, subject to entry visa regulations. Tour registration is in the transit areas of Terminals 2 and 3. There are six tours every day, each lasting 2.5 hours.

From Changi, it is easy to get to the city by the **MRT** subway train, bus, taxi, or the airport shuttle bus, which stops at many downtown hotels. Single journey tickets can be purchased at Changi MRT station, or on board the bus, or you can invest in a public transport pass, available at the Singapore Tourist Pass website. It is about 11 miles (17 km) to downtown, a journey that takes around 1 hour by public transport, or about 25 minutes in a taxi or shuttle bus. There are taxi stands at each of the airport terminals.

Arriving by Train

Rail passengers arrive into Malaysia's Johor Bahru Sentral Railway Station, and have to change trains to cross the causeway to Woodlands Station in north Singapore. From Woodlands Station, there are frequent MRT trains, buses, and taxis to the city center. The opulent **Belmond** Eastern and Oriental Express travels between Bangkok and Singapore, once or twice per month, from February to December.

Arriving by Bus

From Malaysia, direct international buses terminate at various points in Singapore, depending on which company is operating them. Most arrival points are fairly central, and are connected to onwards public transport.

Non-direct buses go from Johor Bahru in Malaysia to Woodlands or Kranji terminals in northern Singapore, from where buses or the MRT go to the city. Passengers have to get off the bus to cross the checkpoint, and board another bus on the Singaporean side. The **SBS Transit** and MRT websites have more information.

Arriving by Sea

Ferries serving the Indonesian Riau Islands, notably Batam and Bintan, arrive at both the **Singapore Cruise Centre** at HarbourFront and the Tanah Merah Ferry Terminal in eastern Singapore. HarbourFront has its own MRT station, while the Tanah Merah Ferry Terminal is served by buses.

Travel Passes

Prepaid **EZ-Link cards** are an excellent way to use Singapore's extensive public transportation system. They are available at any MRT station or 7Eleven store, they can be used on the MRT, LRT (overground light railway), buses and river boats.

One-, two-, or three-day tourist passes are also available from Changi Airport and MRT stations, or at the **Singapore Tourist Pass** website. These allow unlimited travel on the MRT, LRT, and buses.

Getting Around by MRT

The efficient and cheap MRT network operates five lines that run from around 5:40am to midnight. It covers the city center, and reaches the majority of attractions in outlying areas. Location maps and clear signage at every station make it very easy to use.

Getting Around by Bus

Singapore has a good network of clean, air-conditioned buses. Fares vary according to distance and are similar to the price of the MRT. Routes are more complicated to understand than the MRT for short-term visitors, so smartphone transport apps are very useful for planning.

Getting Around by Boat

The 40-minute **Singapore River Cruise**, in old-style bumboats, chugs past Robertson Quay, Clarke Quay, and Boat Quay out into Marina Bay. On tourist boats, a commentary is given via a pre-recorded tape. You can also use an EZ-Link card to pay for a "river taxi" ride, without commentary. These boats can be boarded at several stops along the Singapore River between 8am to 10am, and 5pm to 7pm Monday to Friday.

Getting Around by Taxi

City taxis are relatively inexpensive, although a complex system of peak hour extras and other surcharges can increase fares significantly. Rush hour and rainstorms can make it hard to find a cab. Wait at a taxi stand or use a smartphone app to book a pick up (additional fees may apply). For three or more people, a taxi is the most economical, and the fastest, way to get around the city. **Comfort and CityCab** is Singapore's largest taxi company. The popular **Grab** app provides competition to Uber.

Getting Around by Car

All of the major car-rental companies operate in Singapore, and the rental process is simple for holders of an international driving permit or an English-language license. However, given the ease of public transport, cheap price of taxis, logistics of parking, and various road tolls, renting a car is not hugely popular.

Getting Around by Bicycle

Bicycles come in handy for exploring suburban parks, many linked by the **Park Connector Network (PCN)** of trails, and certain areas such as Pulau Ubin and the Bukit Timah Nature Reserve. However, bike-rental outfits are limited to the East Coast Parkway, coastal parks such as at Changi Beach, Punggol, and Sentosa.

Some effort is being made to create shared bike schemes in specific areas, and Car-Free Sundays are occasionally declared in parts of the city center, but in general cycling along the island's busy highways is not recommended given the almost universal lack of cycle lanes.

Getting Around on Foot

Singapore's city center is compact and easy to explore on foot. Plan longer walking routes carefully, because Singapore's heat and humidity can make even a short stroll tiring during the day. Take plenty of rest breaks, carry enough water to keep rehydrated, and take advantage of the air conditioning in the city's malls when you want to cool down. Night-time walking is pleasant and safe, when streets and parks remain well lit, and it is cooler.

Practical Information

Passports and Visas

Visitors to Singapore require a passport that is valid for at least six months. Most tourists are issued a social visit pass on arrival (for free), valid for up to 30 or 90 days depending on nationality. Citizens of some countries must apply for a visa in advance (costing S$15), through the **Immigration & Checkpoints Authority** website. Many countries, including the **United States**, the **United Kingdom**, and **Australia** have consular representation in Singapore.

Customs Regulations and Immigration

The duty-free allowance is 1 liter of spirits, 1 liter of wine, and 1 liter of beer. No duty-free cigarettes can be brought into Singapore. There is no duty-free allowance for visitors from Malaysia or those out of Singapore for less than 48 hours. Firecrackers, pornography, and pirated CDs/DVDs are banned, as is import of chewing gum for resale. The city's mandatory death sentence for drug offenses applies to foreigners too.

Travel Safety Advice

Visitors can access travel safety advice from the **US Department of State**, the **Australian Department of Foreign Affairs and Trade**, and the **UK Foreign & Commonwealth Office**.

Travel Insurance

All travelers are advised to buy insurance against accidents, illness, theft or loss, and travel delays or cancellations. The excellent healthcare available in Singapore is also very expensive, so it is even more important to have good medical cover.

Health

There are no innoculations for Singapore, but it is recommended that all travelers have up-to-date hepatitis A & B, diphtheria, tetanus, and typhoid shots. Singapore has been free of malaria for decades, but dengue still poses a problem. Using mosquito repellent is advisable in the evenings, and widely available at pharmacies.

Singapore's healthcare is known to be one of the best in the world. The most central hospitals are **Gleneagles Hospital**, **Mount Elizabeth Hospital**, and **Singapore General Hospital**. They all have 24-hour walk-in accident and emergency departments. There are branches of Guardian and Watsons pharmacies in most shopping malls, and some 24-hour pharmacies in the center. Prescriptions from overseas doctors are not accepted. Keep a note of the emergency numbers.

Tap water is usually safe to drink (except on Pulau Ubin), and bottled water is widely available. Food courts are safe, with hygiene standards rated by the government, the highest being "A."

Personal Security

Singapore is an extremely safe city. Laws are strictly enforced, and many minor offenses carry a fine. A foreigner accused of breaking the law may not necessarily have access to legal advice from their home consulate.

Most hotels have in-room safes where you can store personal items, and larger items can often be held in the hotel's main safe.

The **ambulance**, **fire**, and **police** services have dedicated emergency numbers.

Currency and Banking

The Singapore dollar (SGD) is divided into 100 cents. Notes come in denominations of S$2, S$5, S$10, S$20, S$50, and up to S$10,000. Coins come in 5, 10, 20, 50 cent, and S$1 denominations.

Most of the major international banks have branches in Singapore. ATMs that accept cards linked to Cirrus or PLUS networks can be found at banks, shopping malls, and MRT stations. Cards such as Visa, American Express, and Mastercard are widely accepted in shops across Singapore.

Currency can be changed at any hotel or bank, but the best rates are given by the licensed money-changers who operate from booths in shopping centers and commercial hubs. Licensed changers will not charge a commission.

Telephone and Internet

Singapore operates on the GSM network, so most cell phones brought from overseas will work with a local SIM card inserted, although basic 2G phones will not work. Ask your home carrier for the unlock code to use a different SIM card/service. There are three local service providers: **SingTel**, **M1**, and **StarHub**. They all offer prepaid SIM cards and data plans, sold at kiosks, phone stores, 7Elevens, and at Changi Airport. Visitors should note that incoming calls are charged at around 15 cents per minute with most prepaid deals.

Major international hotels provide in-room, high-speed Internet access. There are free Wi-Fi hotspots in the city via the Wireless@SG network, which requires users to register with a foreign or local mobile number. Many shopping malls offer free Wi-Fi.

Postal Services

Efficient mail-and-package handling from post offices and kiosks at MRT stations and shopping malls is provided by **SingPost**.

TV, Radio, and Newspapers

Singapore has two local TV channels in English. **Channel NewsAsia** offers CNN-style rolling news, while **MediaCorp Channel 5** shows lifestyle shows. The national daily broadsheet is *The Straits Times*. *TODAY* is a free English-language commuter paper.

Travelers with Disabilities

Visitors with mobility issues will find Singapore well equipped for their needs. Persons with disabilities and their primary caregivers get free or discounted entry to national museums. The MRT stations have elevators, and wheelchair-friendly taxis can be booked from the main taxi operators.The **Singapore Disabled People's Association** offers good, up-to-date information.

DIRECTORY

PASSPORTS AND VISAS

Australian High Commission
W www.australia.org.sg

British High Commission
W ukinsingapore.fco.gov.uk

Immigration & Checkpoints Authority
W ica.gov.sg

US Embassy
W singapore.usembassy.gov

TRAVEL SAFETY ADVICE

Australian Department of Foreign Trade and Affairs
W dfat.gov.au
W smartraveller.gov.au

UK Foreign & Commonwealth Office
W gov.uk/foreign-travel-advice

US Department of State
W travel.state.gov

HEALTH

Gleneagles Hospital
W gleneagles.com.sg

Mount Elizabeth Hospital
W mountelizabeth.com.sg

Singapore General Hospital
W sgh.com.sg

PERSONAL SECURITY

Ambulance and Fire
995

Police
999

TELEPHONE AND INTERNET

M1
W www.m1.com.sg

SingTel
W info.singtel.com

StarHub
W www.starhub.com

POSTAL SERVICES

SingPost
W singpost.com

TV, RADIO, AND NEWSPAPERS

Channel NewsAsia
W channelnewsasia.com

MediaCorp Channel 5
W tv.toggle.sg/channel5

The Straits Times
W straitstimes.com

TODAY
W todayonline.com

TRAVELERS WITH DISABILITIES

Singapore Disabled People's Association
W dpa.org.sg

Sources of Information

The **Singapore Tourism Board** has 20 offices abroad, mainly located in Asia. They have a toll-free number for use in Singapore, and their information-packed website is constantly updated with new events.

Services offered by the main **Singapore Visitor Centre** include the sale of tours, tickets for attractions and events, and Singapore Tourist Passes. The **Chinatown Visitor Centre** offers useful information and walking tours. Hotels provide free maps of the city. These can also be picked up on arrival at Changi Airport.

Available for free at some malls, cafés, and bars, the **SGNow** magazine has reviews of the latest eating, shopping, and entertainment venues. Other useful websites include **hungrygowhere** for restaurant reviews, and **City Nomads** for news of the latest events, eateries, hotels, and shops.

Opening Hours

Banks are open between 9:30am and 3pm Monday–Friday and until 1pm on Saturday. Shops and malls are generally open 10am–10pm, and several stay open till 11pm at weekends. Major museums are open every day from 10am–7pm, and some have extended hours on Friday nights until 9pm. Many of the smaller museums are shut on Mondays.

Time Difference

Singapore is 8 hours ahead of GMT, 12 or 13 hours ahead of New York, and 2 or 3 hours behind Sydney. There is no daylight saving time in Singapore; sunrise and sunset are around 7am and 7pm all year round.

Electrical Appliances

Singapore's electricity is modeled on the British system of 220–240 volts. Power plugs are also of the British three-pin type. Hotels usually have adaptors they can loan guests.

Weather

Singapore's temperature remains fairly constant throughout the year, with an average high of 31° C (88° F) and relative humidity of 85 per cent. Rainfall is highest November–January and lowest June–July. Peak travel season is from mid-December through to the Chinese New Year in January/February.

Tours

The **SIA Hop-On Bus** has four routes traveling between more than 20 tourist hotspots, with guided commentary in 12 languages. Tickets are valid for 24 hours, and buses operate between 9am and 6.30pm.

Trishaw Uncle offer 45-minute tricycle tours around the Singapore River and Little India.

The Original Singapore Walks conduct themed walking tours through ethnic neighborhoods with expert guides who give details about local customs, history, and heritage. Different walks are scheduled on different days (except Sundays and public holidays). No reservations are required – just show up and pay the tour guide.

A variety of bus tours and packages is offered by **DUCK & HIPPO Tours**, including a 1-hour city-and-river tour on an amphibious vehicle.

Shopping

With more than 100 malls, ethnic neighborhood stores, and a thriving home-grown design movement, Singapore is a shopper's paradise. The city center is thick with shiny malls selling big-name fashion brands, and the suburbs have large shopping centers of their own. Luxury malls are concentrated along **Orchard Road** (see pp94–9) and around **Marina Bay** (see pp28–9). Local designers can be found across the city in orchardgateway, Far East Plaza, and Orchard Central malls.

Little India (see pp78–85), **Chinatown** (see pp70–77) and **Kampong Glam** (see pp78–85) feature specialist Indian, Chinese, and Malay shops selling clothing, fabrics, souvenirs, and crafts. For arts and antiques, **Dempsey Road** (see p104) has numerous retailers.

The 7 per cent Goods and Services Tax (GST) can be reclaimed by visitors spending at least S$100 a day at participating stores. Upon purchase, ask the shop assistant for a GST Refund form. Present the form with your receipt and the goods purchased at GST refund desks at your point of departure.

Where to Eat

Singapore is renowned for its food, and eating out is a national pastime. There are restaurants to suit every taste and budget, including 29 with Michelin stars – two of which are humble hawker stands. The multicultural society means that Indian, Malay, Peranakan, various regional Chinese cuisines, and Singaporean fusion dishes are island-wide staples. Hawker centers (also known as food centers, or as food courts) offer the full range of local specialties under one roof at rock-bottom prices. Upscale restaurants are found in luxury hotels and **Marina Bay Sands** *(see p28)*. Vegetarian food is easy to find. A lot of Western restaurants and fast-food chains have franchises in Singapore as well.

Many of Singapore's formal restaurants close between mealtimes. Inexpensive restaurants seldom accept reservations, but for more upmarket places a booking is highly recommended, particularly at weekends.

Most restaurant and bar bills will add a 10 per cent service charge and 7 per cent GST. Tipping is not practiced in Singapore, but many diners leave small change for the server (although not in hawker centers).

Eating out with children is common in Singapore, except in top-end establishments, and many restaurants provide high chairs, changing facilities, child-friendly utensils and kids' menus. The climate makes outdoor dining ubiquitous, and so families will find a wide choice of restaurants with gardens and play areas for kids. The website **hungrygowhere** provides a useful, quick way to book a restaurant.

Where to Stay

Singapore has a range of accommodation to suit every pocket. Superluxury hotels can be found throughout the city, and especially on Sentosa, while major international chains and sleek business hotels are concentrated in the central city and financial districts, and along Orchard Road. A number of operators have serviced apartments for long-term guests – a good option for families. Boutique hotels are becoming increasingly popular, often occupying heritage buildings, and can be great value. The majority of economical hostels are found in Little India, Chinatown, and Kampong Glam. Although budget travelers will find that rooms are not as cheap as in the rest of Asia, the standards of cleanliness and amenities are much higher. Because Singapore is so compact, wherever you stay will feel fairly central.

Rates and Booking

Singapore's hotels enjoy high occupancy rates year-round, so reserving early is recommended. If you arrive without a reservation, try the **Singapore Hotel Association**, which operates counters at all Changi Airport arrival halls. Most hotels offer their best rates online.

Because Singapore hosts business events and conventions year-round, there is no "peak season". Top rates apply around Christmas and rates also increase during major sporting events or trade conventions.

DIRECTORY

SOURCES OF INFORMATION

Chinatown Visitor Centre
Kreta Ayer Square
🆆 chinatown.sg

City Nomads
🆆 citynomads.com/singapore

hungrygowhere
🆆 hungrygowhere.com

Singapore Tourism Board
📞 1800-736-2000
🆆 yoursingapore.com

SGNow
🆆 sg.asia-city.com

Singapore Visitor Centre
216 Orchard Road
📞 6736-2000

TOURS

SIA Hop-On Bus
🆆 siahopon.com

Trishaw Uncle
🆆 trishawuncle.com.sg

The Original Singapore Walks
🆆 journeys.com.sg/singaporewalks/index.asp

DUCK & HIPPO Tours
🆆 ducktours.com.sg

RATES AND BOOKING

Singapore Hotel Association
🆆 stayinsingapore.com

Places to Stay

PRICE CATEGORIES

For a standard double room per night (with breakfast if included), taxes and extra charges.

$ under S$200 $$ S$200–400 $$$ over S$400

Super Luxury Hotels

Capella Singapore

MAP S3 ■ 1 The Knolls, Sentosa ■ 6377-8888 ■ www.capellahotels.com/singapore ■ $$$

Combining lovely colonial architecture and modern resort-style rooms, the Capella Singapore offers an award-winning spa and can arrange tours or sailing trips. The swimming pool is beautiful, and the elevated views are sublime.

Fairmont Singapore

MAP M1 ■ 80 Bras Basah Rd ■ 6339-7777 ■ www.fairmont.com/singapore ■ $$$

Each of the Fairmont's 769 luxuriously appointed rooms and suites is its own private sanctuary. The hotel offers a wealth of facilities and world-class pampering experiences, including an award-winning spa.

Four Seasons Hotel

MAP A4 ■ 190 Orchard Boulevard ■ 6734-1110 ■ www.fourseasons.com ■ $$$

This 20-story building is just a jog away from the Botanic Gardens. Rooms have charming continental decor and comfortable beds. The One-Ninety restaurant does a great Sunday Champagne lunch.

Fullerton Hotel

MAP M3 ■ 1 Fullerton Square ■ 6733-8388 ■ www.fullertonhotel.com ■ $$$

Converted from the former General Post Office, this gracious landmark has guest rooms with high ceilings and long windows. The views are spectacular, overlooking the colonial district or Marina Bay, depending on your room.

Goodwood Park Hotel

MAP B3 ■ 22 Scotts Rd ■ 6737-7411 ■ www.goodwoodparkhotel.com ■ $$$

Built in 1900 as a club for German expatriates, Goodwood Park was converted into a hotel in 1929. The hotel tower is a national monument. Rooms are classic in decor, with contemporary amenities. The dining options are excellent.

Mandarin Oriental

MAP N2 ■ 5 Raffles Avenue ■ 6338-0066 ■ www.mandarinoriental.com ■ $$$

The slick and polished Mandarin has a black marble lobby and classic Asian art and furnishings. It is close to conference venues and the Central Business District.

Raffles Hotel

MAP M1 ■ 1 Beach Rd ■ 6337-1886 ■ www.singapore.raffles.com ■ $$$

Raffles is pure romance and nostalgia, with rooms restored to resemble the hotel's 1910s heyday. Award-winning dining options adds to its appeal.

Ritz-Carlton, Millenia Singapore

MAP P2 ■ 7 Raffles Ave ■ 6337-8888 ■ www.ritzcarlton.com ■ $$$

Located near convention facilities and the Central Business District, this hotel is typically booked by high-profile business guests. Contemporary art pieces grace public areas and rooms. Marble bathrooms have huge tubs and panoramic views.

Shangri-La Hotel

MAP A3 ■ 22 Orange Grove Rd ■ 6737-3644 ■ www.shangri-la.com ■ $$

With 15 acres (6 ha) of sprawling gardens, the Shangri-La is an oasis in the city. Guests can choose from three styles of accommodation: the classically elegant rooms of the Valley Wing, the urban resort feel of the Garden Wing, or the stylish, contemporary rooms Ein the Tower Wing.

Sofitel Sentosa Resort & Spa

MAP S3 ■ 2 Bukit Manis Rd ■ 6708-8310 ■ www.sofitel-singapore-sentosa.com ■ $$$

Home to So SPA by Sofitel, this French-inspired resort is set amid lush greenery and tropical fish ponds. Ideal both for couples and families, most rooms promise a garden view. ilLido at the Cliff restaurant has superb Italian cuisine.

The St. Regis Singapore
MAP S3 ▪ 29 Tanglin Rd ▪ 6506-6888 ▪ www. stregis.com/singapore ▪ $$$
The exclusive St. Regis is famous for its superb butler service. The truly luxurious guest rooms and suites have beautiful hand-painted silk wall coverings, designer upholstery, and French marble bathrooms. Facilities include the award-winning Remede spa, a state-of-the-art fitness center, and an outdoor spa pool.

Boutique Hotels

Amoy
MAP L4 ▪ 76 Telok Ayer St ▪ 6580-2888 ▪ www. stayfareast.com ▪ $$
Few hotels can boast a building like the Fuk Tai Chi museum (see p77) as an entrance. This clever shophouse conversion incorporates the museum as well as a warren of 37 rooms, some with suitably Chinese decorative motifs.

The Club
MAP K4 ▪ 28 Ann Siang Rd ▪ 6808-2188 ▪ www. theclub.com.sg ▪ $$
The 20-rooms in this hotel are intermingled with two restaurants, a basement lounge and a rooftop bar. Rooms have spacious bathrooms and luxurious furnishings

and bedding, as well as exclusive toiletries. All suites have large balconies overlooking the street below.

Hotel 1929
MAP J4 ▪ 50 Keong Saik Rd ▪ 6347-1929 ▪ www. hotel1929.com ▪ $$
Contemporary chic design is used to maximize space and brighten up this little hotel in a renovated shophouse located in the heart of Chinatown. Rooms are small.

Hôtel Vagabond
MAP G3 ▪ 39 Syed Alwi Rd ▪ 6291-6677 ▪ www. hotelvagabondsingapore. com ▪ $$
This high-concept boutique hotel has rooms that are quirky, vibrant, and chic. Some of the boudoirs have terraces, and the restaurant and bar are acclaimed. Keep an eye out for the giant brass rhino and elephant.

Link Hotel
MAP T3 ▪ 50 Tiong Bahru Rd ▪ 6622-8585 ▪ www. linkhotel.com.sg ▪ $$
This unique Art Deco property is the result of the government's first public housing project. Located in a charming old suburb not far from Chinatown, the hotel has contemporary interiors with lively ethnic themes.

Naumi Hotel
MAP G6 ▪ 41 Seah St ▪ 6403-6000 ▪ www. naumihotel.com ▪ $$
This stylish property is part business hotel – with its 24-hour butler service – and part

boutique hotel, being smaller and more intimate than most. Rooms and facilities at the Naumi focus on state-of-the-art technology and edgy design.

The Scarlet Hotel
MAP K5 ▪ 33 Erskine Rd ▪ 6511-3333 ▪ www. thescarlethotel.com ▪ $$
An experience for the senses, the Scarlet Hotel is swathed in deep velvet, silk, and satin, with bespoke furnishings and glistening lacquer accents. The suites are cosy and intimate, but the standard and deluxe rooms are tiny, so it may not be ideal for those staying more than a few days.

Business Hotels

Destination Singapore
MAP H5 ▪ 700 Beach Rd ▪ 6679-2000 ▪ www. parkhotelgroup.com ▪ $
This ten-storey hotel has surprisingly spacious, comfortable rooms for the price, as well as excellent views of the Singapore Flyer and Marina Bay's towers from its rooftop pool.

Crowne Plaza Changi Airport Hotel
MAP V2 ▪ 75 Airport Boulevard ▪ 8235-5300 ▪ www.crowneplaza.com ▪ $$
This is Singapore's first international business hotel to be located at the airport, which is still close enough to make quick trips into town. It is also near the Singapore Expo and the East Coast industrial parks.

InterContinental

MAP G5 ▪ 80 Middle Rd ▪ 6338-7600 ▪ www.intercontinental.com ▪ $$

Built atop a cluster of pre-war shophouses, the hotel has absorbed these original structures as well as local style into its decor. It is located above an MRT station not far from the Suntec Convention Center.

M Hotel

MAP K6 ▪ 81 Anson Rd ▪ 6224-1133 ▪ www.m-hotel.com ▪ $$

One of the very few international business-class hotels located inside the Shenton Way financial district, M Hotel caters working guests, with a business center and office suites on level 8. Weekend guests can enjoy good discounts.

Marina Mandarin

MAP N2 ▪ 6 Raffles Boulevard ▪ 6845-1000 ▪ www.meritushotels.com ▪ $$

Built around an atrium lobby, this business hotel is connected to the Marina Square shopping mall. The views from the rooms that face the bay are terrific.

Sheraton Towers

MAP C2 ▪ 39 Scotts Rd ▪ 6737-6888 ▪ www.sheratonsingapore.com ▪ $$

Centrally located, this 420-room hotel is known for its outstanding quality and personalized butler service. Equipped with modern amenities and conveniences, the hotel's elegant rooms offer contemporary comfort and stylish sophistication.

Conrad Centennial

MAP N2 ▪ 2 Temasek Boulevard ▪ 6334-8888 ▪ www.conradhotels.com ▪ $$

The Conrad is ideally situated for business travelers. Its guest rooms are located in two towers and feature state-of-the-art communications facilities. They are supported by conference rooms and a business center.

Grand Hyatt

MAP B4 ▪ 10 Scotts Rd ▪ 6738-1234 ▪ www.singapore.grand.hyatt.com ▪ $$$

The check-in area here is located out of view of the main doors. While the Grand Rooms are larger, the Terrace Wing rooms have bright workspaces with Internet and entertainment options.

Marina Bay Sands

MAP N4 ▪ 10 Bayfront Avenue ▪ 6688-8868 ▪ www.marinabaysands.com ▪ $$$

The leading resort destination in Asia, this hotel features convention and exhibition facilities, 2,560 rooms and suites, two theaters, the rooftop Sands SkyPark, and world-class restaurants. Completing the line-up of attractions is the ArtScience Museum at Marina Bay Sands.

Singapore Marriott Tang Plaza Hotel

MAP B4 ▪ 320 Orchard Rd ▪ 6735-5800 ▪ www.marriott.com ▪ $$$

Located in the heart of the city's business, shopping, and entertainment district, the Singapore Marriott offers both business and leisure travelers the highest level of luxury.

Singapore Marriott South Beach

MAP N2 ▪ 30 Beach Rd ▪ 6818-1888 ▪ www.marriott.com ▪ $$$

The South Beach has splendid views and is bang next to Suntec City. Rooms are designed by Philippe Starck, plus there are two infinity pools in the Sky Gardens and super chic dining.

Family Hotels

YWCA Fort Canning Lodge

MAP E6 ▪ 6 Fort Canning Rd ▪ 6338-4222 ▪ www.ywcafclodge.org.sg ▪ $

Like the YMCA close by, the YWCA enjoys a central location. The well-equipped rooms and family suites are a good size with views of the pool or the park. There is a café that is open all day and a self-service laundry; the staff are friendly and helpful.

YMCA International House

MAP E6 ▪ 1 Orchard Rd ▪ 6336-6000 ▪ www.ymcaih.com.sg ▪ $

Of the several YMCAs in Singapore, International House is hard to beat for location – just a couple of minutes' walk from the National Museum and other historic sights as well as bustling Orchard Road. It also has a café, a pool, and a gym. The rooms here range from four-bed dormitories to junior suites.

Holiday Inn Singapore Orchard City Centre

MAP D5 ■ 11 Cavenagh Rd ■ 6733-8333 ■ www.ihg.com/holidayinn ■ $$

This hotel has rooms that are large, clean, and well-equipped with fridges and coffee-making facilities. There is a decent breakfast buffet, service standards are high, and there is a rooftop pool and a fitness centre. Two restaurants and a bar complete the package. Kids can stay for free in their parents' room.

Orchard Parade Hotel

MAP A4 ■ 1 Tanglin Rd ■ 6737-1133 ■ www.stayfareast.com ■ $$

This is a great location at a good price. The hotel has a lovely pool, good laundry facilities, and family studios with lounge and dining areas.

Parkroyal

MAP H5 ■ 7500 Beach Rd ■ 6505-5666 ■ www.parkroyalhotels.com ■ $$

Close to Arab Street, the Parkroyal has good facilities at a reasonable price. Rooms are slightly bland but clean. Some interconnecting rooms are available, too. The huge rooftop pool is popular with children.

Siloso Beach Resort

MAP S3 ■ 51 Imbiah Walk, Sentosa ■ 6722-3310 ■ www.siloso beachresort.com ■ $$

The glass walls of this resort offer great views of the beach, and it is just a short walk to the sea. There are one- and two-bedroom villas, as well as the rooms in the main hotel. The leisure facilities are excellent, and there is a waterfall pool.

Village Hotel Bugis

MAP G5 ■ 390 Victoria St ■ 6297-2828 ■ www.village hotelbugis.com.sg ■ $$

This bustling hotel is family-friendly to the extent that it even has themed rooms for kids, with child-friendly toiletries and cartoon wallpaper. It is centrally located on the edge of Kampong Glam.

York Hotel

MAP C4 ■ 21 Mount Elizabeth ■ 6737-0511 ■ www.yorkhotel.com.sg ■ $$

A 10-minute walk from Orchard Road, the York has notably spacious rooms with neutral furnishings. There are four categories of room designed to accommodate families, a pool, and in-house dining.

Festive Hotel

MAP S3 ■ Resort World Sentosa ■ 6577-8899 ■ www.rwsentosa.com ■ $$$

This hotel caters for children just as much as adults, with welcome packs and candy at reception and specially tailored bathrobes for the kids. The deluxe family king rooms are separated into two areas with a king-sized bed for parents and a loft bed that youngsters will love.

Fraser Place

MAP J2 ■ 11 Unity St ■ 6736-4800 ■ www.frasers hospitality.com ■ $$$

For stays of more than a week, Fraser Place has well-equipped one-, two-, and three-bedroom apartments right on the riverfront. There is a playground and a pool with a supermarket and cafés nearby.

Shangri-La's Rasa Sentosa Resort

MAP S3 ■ 101 Siloso Rd ■ 6275-0100 ■ www.shangri-la.com ■ $$$

The only beach front hotel in Singapore is an attractive choice for families. The children's club features a tree-house slide and a range of organized activities. There is also a children's pool, with water slides. All rooms have a balcony overlooking the hills or the South China Sea.

Value-for-Money Hotels

Hotel Bencoolen

MAP F5 ■ 47 Bencoolen St ■ 6336-0822 ■ www.hotelbencoolen.com ■ $

Only a few minutes' walk away from Orchard Road and Little India, the Bencoolen's location makes it a good choice. The rooms are clean and equipped with TVs and coffee-making facilities. Breakfast is a Western-style buffet, and there is a modest rooftop pool.

The Inn at Temple Street

MAP K4 ■ 36 Temple St ■ 6221-5333 ■ www.theinn.com.sg ■ $

Right in the heart of the Chinatown Conservation Area, this award-winning inn takes up a row of five renovated shophouses. It is not strong on modern comforts and the rooms are small, but it has a charm that is unusual at this price.

For a key to hotel price categories see p114

Innotel

MAP K1 ▪ 11 Penang Lane ▪ 6327-2727 ▪ www. innotelhotel.com.sg ▪ $
Just a stone's throw from Orchard Road, this compact hotel features contemporary decor throughout. There are few special amenities although breakfast is available, usually as a paid extra.

Keong Saik Hotel

MAP J4 ▪ 69 Keong Saik Rd ▪ 6223-0660 ▪ www. keongsaikhotel.com.sg ▪ $
Another boutique hotel built from old shop-houses, with small, sparsely furnished rooms. The hardwood floors are clean, and decorative molding surrounds windows overlooking an attractive Chinatown lane.

Robertson Quay Hotel

MAP J2 ▪ 15 Merbau Rd ▪ 6735-3333 ▪ www. robertsonquayhotel.com. sg ▪ $
This hotel has same great location as the Fraser Place Suites (see p117), but at a lower price. The rooms and bathrooms are basic; the best and quietest rooms face the river. There is a small pool on the roof and an outside bar, and the restaurants and bars of Robertson Quay are just moments away.

Strand Hotel

MAP F5 ▪ 25 Bencoolen St ▪ 6338-1866 ▪ www. strandhotel.com.sg ▪ $
The Strand does not look like a budget place. Rooms are large and colorful with a range of deluxe and family rooms, which can accommodate up to seven guests. "Special" rooms are vividly decorated.

Summer View Hotel

MAP F5 ▪ 173 Bencoolen St ▪ 6338-1122 ▪ www. accorhotels.com.sg ▪ $
This inexpensive hotel is surrounded by a host of attractions. It has all the basics – breakfast buffet, cable TV, Internet, and coffee-making facilities, but no pool.

Albert Court Village Hotel

MAP F4 ▪ 180 Albert St ▪ 6339-3939 ▪ www. village hotelalbertcourt. com.sg ▪ $$
This lovely little hotel is decorated with Peranakan textiles, carved wood furnishings, and trad-itional floral tiles. There is a gym, Jacuzzis, and a coffee shop, while the central courtyard is a popular place to hang out.

Hotel Grand Central

MAP D5 ▪ 22 Cavenagh Rd ▪ 6737-9944 ▪ www. grandcentral.com.sg ▪ $$
Nowhere else in the city will you get such a great location for the price. Do not expect much in the way of facilities, but this place may appeal to visitors who use a hotel as a crash pad and want to be close to Orchard Road.

Lloyd's Inn

MAP J1 ▪ 2 Lloyd Rd ▪ 6737-7309 ▪ www. lloydsinn.com ▪ $$
This intimate, sociable hotel has an excellent location near Orchard Road. The roof terrace is lovely, and minimalist design throughout makes the most of light and air. Although facilities are limited, they do include a dipping pool surrounded with lush foliage.

M Social

MAP T3 ▪ 90 Robertson Quay ▪ 6206-1888 ▪ www.msocial.com.sg ▪ $$
Trendy and techy, this hotel sports cutting-edge design by Philippe Starck, with contrasting textiles and tiles. The social aspect is played out in the arty Asian-fusion resto-bar, Beasts & Butterflies, which has communal tables. Rooms are quirky yet sophisticated.

Peninsula Excelsior Hotel

MAP L2 ▪ 5 Coleman St ▪ 6337-2200 ▪ www. ytchotels.com.sg ▪ $$
The result of a merger of the Excelsior and Peninsula hotels gives you twice the facilities and two rooms facing Marina Bay – you will not get a better view at the price.

RELC International Hotel

MAP A2 ▪ 30 Orange Grove Rd ▪ 6885-7888 ▪ www.relcih.com.sg ▪ $$
RELC offers an excellent combination of location and facilities at a very good price. There is a decent range of rooms and prices, but all are reasonably large and equipped with balconies, cable TV, fridge, and coffee-making facilities. The free breakfast isn't brilliant, but there are plenty of tempting options on Orchard Road, just 10 minutes' walk away.

Cheap Sleeps

Backpacker Cozy Corner Guest House
MAP G5 ■ 490 North Bridge Rd ■ 6338-8826 ■ www.cozycornerguest.com ■ $
Single and double-bed rooms are small, simple, and very clean, but none has an en suite bathroom. Dorm rooms are available, and facilities include Internet, laundry service, kitchenette, and sundeck.

Beary Best! Hostel
MAP K4 ■ 16 Upper Cross St ■ 6222-4957 ■ www.bearybesthostel.com ■ $
This hostel in Chinatown provides a cozy ambience and useful facilities. It is also great value for money, with a location that is literally only a few steps away from Chinatown MRT station.

Betel Box
MAP T2 ■ 200 Joo Chiat Rd ■ 6247-7340 ■ www.betelbox.com ■ $
All the rooms in this hostel are equipped with free Wi-Fi. The modern Asian decor reflects the building's heritage as a former shophouse. The Joo Chiat area in which it is located is home to a number of eateries.

Fernloft Singapore Chinatown
MAP K4 ■ #02–92 Block 5 Banda St ■ 6323-3221 ■ www.fernloft.com ■ $
A terrific location in Chinatown adds to the appeal of this guesthouse. It has private rooms and dorms, all with shared bath. The owners also operate a great hostel in a quiet neighborhood in the suburb of East Coast.

hangout@mt.emily
MAP E4 ■ 10A Upper Wilkie Rd ■ 6438-5588 ■ www.hangouthotels.com ■ $
Designed for those image-conscious budget travelers, hangout has small, spartan, bright rooms with a funky feel and contemporary decor. Private rooms with en suites are available.

The Hive Backpackers' Hostel
MAP G2 ■ 624 Serangoon Rd ■ www.hivesg.com ■ $
Not quite centrally located, but clean and safe, this hostel has private rooms – some with en suite bathrooms – and dorms, which are all air-conditioned. Breakfast is included, and a lounge offers cable TV plus free Internet access.

Hotel Re!
MAP J4 ■ 175A Chin Swee Rd ■ 6827-8288 ■ www.hotelre.com.sg ■ $
The retro furnishings and psychedelic decor (including glittery mosaic bath tiles) of this hotel attract a younger clientele. Located only a 15-minute walk from Chinatown and with friendly staff, the Hotel Re! is a good-value option.

Hotel Yan
MAP H2 ■ 162 Tyrwhitt Rd ■ 6805-1955 ■ www.hotel-yan.com ■ $
Backpackers can up the budget a bit to enjoy industrial-chic in this cozy hotel not far from Little India and Kampong Glam. Rooms here are small but well equipped, with picture windows and complimentary snacks and toiletries.

The InnCrowd Backpackers' Hostel
MAP F4 ■ 73 Dunlop St ■ 6296-9169 ■ www.the-inncrowd.com ■ $
A well-planned place, this Little India hostel is clean and spacious. All the air-conditioned dormitories and private rooms have access to bathrooms, a kitchenette, an on-site pub serving cheap beer, Internet facilities, a travel library, and a rooftop sundeck.

Met A Space Pod
MAP L3 ■ 51 Boat Quay ■ 6635-2694 ■ www.meta-spacepod.com.sg ■ $
This hostel has high-tech, capsule-style beds which give you the feeling of sleeping inside your own cylinder within a space probe. Thankfully, the kitchen, bathrooms and breakfasts are much more down-to-earth.

Perak Hotel
MAP F4 ■ 12 Perak Rd ■ 6299-7733 ■ www.peraklodge.net ■ $
The friendly front-desk staff make guests feel at home in this small guesthouse in Little India. It has clean private rooms, with dressing tables, closets, and en suite bathrooms. An unfussy café serves free breakfast for guests.

Sleepy Kiwi
MAP H5 ■ 55 Bussorah St ■ www.sleepykiwi.com.sg ■ $
Located in Kampong Glam, this charming guesthouse is in a traditional building that is surrounded by late-night cafés. It has private rooms as well as dorms. Facilities include a café, Wi-Fi, free breakfast, kitchenette, and lounge.

For a key to hotel price categories see p114

Spread Heading

Acknowledgments

Authors

Susy Atkinson is a writer and freelance journalist. She has traveled widely in Asia and contributed to several travel guides. Susy currently lives in Singapore.

Jennifer Eveland has lived in Bangkok and Singapore since 1998. She has authored a number of travel guides to the area, and contributed to a range of publications on topics as varied as travel, fashion, finance, and politics.

Additional contributor
Vanessa Betts

Publishing Director Georgina Dee

Publisher Vivien Antwi

Design Director Phil Ormerod

Editorial Ankita Awasthi Tröger, Michelle Crane, Rachel Fox, Maresa Manera, Freddie Marriage, Sally Schafer, Farah Sheikh, Hollie Teague, Rachel Thompson

Cover Design Richard Czapnik

Design Tessa Bindloss, Bharti Karakoti

Commissioned Photography Rough Guides / Simon Bracken, Tony Souter

Picture Research Susie Peachey, Ellen Root, Lucy Sienkowska

Cartography Reetu Pandey, Casper Morris, James Macdonald

DTP Jason Little

Production Luca Bazzoli

Factchecker Richard Lim

Proofreader Clare Peel

Indexer Helen Peters

First edition created by Quadrum Solutions, Mumbai

Picture Credits

The publisher would like to thank the following for their kind permission to reproduce their photographs:
Key: a-above; b-below/bottom; c-centre; f-far; l-left; r-right; t-top

123RF.com: Pisit Khambubpha 83b; saiko3p 71b; Ignasi Such 73cl.

Acid Bar: 56c.

Alamy Stock Photo: 509 collection 44tl; Artokoloro Quint Lox Limited 36tr; Alan Keith Beastall 31tl; Stephen Belcher 79tr; dbimages / Betty Johnson 45cl; Paul Dymond 26cr; economic images 93cr; Robert Fried 63br;

imageBROKER / Peter Schickert 22-3, / Valentin Wolf 2tl, 8-9; John Warburton-Lee Photography / Andrew Watson 4cr; JTB Media Creation, Inc. 85cla; Jason Knott 27tl; Art Kowalsky 43cra; Jon Lord 97cl; David Parker 31bl; Sean Pavone 4b; pbpvision 21br; Simon Reddy 77tr, 86-7; REUTERS / Roger Bacon 67cla; Prasit Rodphan 28-9; Peter Schickert 4t; Fedor Selivanov 80c; Neil Setchfield 3tl, 68-9; Lee Snider 16br; Antony Souter 17tl, 17br, 19br, 76tc; Kumar Sriskandan 20cl; Stock Connection Blue / Dallas and John Heaton 4clb; Steve Vidler 61cla; Maximilian Weinzierl 1, 32-3; xPACIFICA 57br.

Asian Civilisations Museum: 14clb, 39c, 43br.

Bugis+: 92b.

Chinatown Heritage Centre: Victor Chick Wh 38br, 71tr.

Dreamstime.com: Ahau1969 25cr; Ake1150sb 6br; Arndale 4cla; Boggy 70tl; Boule13 11c; Cristinnastoian 11tr; Dolphfyn 61tr; Eugenelow 90b; Evolution1088 51tr, 94c; Gianguyen189 89b; Gnohz 4cl; Goinyk 11cla; Haslinda 24bl; Iorboaz 10bl, 80tl; Irynarasko 30-1; Jimmytst 46tr, 62cla; Jirousek 101tl; Joshelerry 27br; Kheng1987 25tl; Korkorkorpai 11clb; Kryu 15crb; Kuba 101br; Leesniderphotoimages 54tl; Leungchopan 14-5; Louisescott 21crb; Minyun9260 24-5, 96c; Mvtmdn 25bc; Naruto4836 63tl; Platongkoh 28crb; Prestonia 12cla; Pusulan 7cl; Quanstills 40b; Ravijohnsmith 10cl; Ronniechua 20-1; Saiko3p 15bl; Salparadis 47c; Samanthatan 44b; Schlenger86 100cla; Sepavo 4crb; Siblingstudio 77c; Sosharp 2tr, 34-5; Pu Sulan 26bl; Svanhorn4245 89tl; Wai Chung Tang 91cl; Tang90246 65br; Tanteckken 26-7; Tktktk 6cla; Tongtranson 7tr, 66b; Toomtamgeo 46-7.

FLPA: ImageBroker 24cb.

Getty Images: AFP / Roslan Rahman 67br, / Roslan Rahman 96tl; Arterra / UIG 72br; Atlantide Phototravel 62br; Gonzalo Azumendi 19tl, 81bl; Allan Baxter 10crb; Bloomberg / Nicky Loh 38cla; John Seaton Callahan 3tr, 106-7; Angelo Cavalli 76clb; Wendy Chan 74cla; Corbis / Columbia Pictures / Sunset Boulevard 37tr; DEA / G. Dagli Orti 36b; EyeEm / Chee Hoe Fong 66tc; EyeEm / Fumiko Mizuno 104clb; fiftymm99 50b, 66cla; Manfred Gottschalk 16-7; Dave and Les Jacobs 41tr; Jean-Pierre Lescourret 95tl; Calvin Chan Wai Meng 72t; Thomas Müller 42t; Popperfoto / Paul Popper 37cr, 45tr; robertharding / Amanda Hall 10cb; Baerbel Schmidt 60tl; simonlong 60b, 74br; sivarock 102c; Chan Srithaweeporn 64t; ullstein bild / Dagmar Scherf 84bl.

Goodwood Park Hotel: 96b.

Invade Industry PTE LTD: 51cl.

iStockphoto.com: Roman Babakin 54-5; Delpixart 20br.

Loof/The Lo & Behold Group: 57cl.

Mandarin Oriental: 49t.

Marina Bay Sands Pte Ltd: Rory Daniel 56t; Eyeamseeingthings / Koh Sze Kiat 28bl.

National Gallery Singapore: 55cr.

National Heritage Board, Singapore: Collection of Indian Heritage Centre 82cb.

Courtesy of National Museum of Singapore, National Heritage Board: 10ca, 12bl, 12crb, 13tl, 13crb, 39t.

NParks: 103cl.

Open Door Policy (Bless Inc. Asia Private Limited): 105cra.

PAssion WaVe@Marina Bay: Zane Lee 53tr.

Potato Head Folk Theatre: 75cr.

Raffles Hotel/FRHI Hotels & Resorts: 30ca, 30bl, 31crb, 59c, 90tl.

Resorts World Sentosa: 11br, 32bl, 33crb, 33bl, 52cb, 53bl.

Rex Shutterstock: Richard Sowersby 88tl.

The Ritz-Carlton, Millenia Sinagpore: 59t.

Robert Harding Picture Library: Christian Kober 16cla.

Shanghai Tang: martinstudio 98t.

Shangri-La Hotel, Singapore: 99clb.

Sofitel Singapore Sentosa Resort & Spa: 48tc.

Spa Esprit Dempsey: 48br.

Sultan Mosque: 18cla, 18crb.

Sun Yat Sen Nanyang Memorial Hall: National Heritage Board Singapore 102t.

The White Rabbit/ The Lo & Behold Group: 58br.

Wild Wild Wet - NTUC Club: 52tl.

Cover
Front and spine: **4Corners:** Maurizio Rellini.
Back: **Dreamstime.com:** Ronniechua.

Pull Out Map Cover
4Corners: Maurizio Rellini.

All other images © Dorling Kindersley
For further information see:
www.dkimages.com

As a guide to abbreviations in visitor information blocks: **Adm** = *admission charge;* **DA** = *disabled access;* **D** = *dinner;* **L** = *lunch.*

Penguin Random House

Printed and bound in China

First American edition, 2009
Published in the United States by
DK Publishing, 345 Hudson Street,
New York, New York 10014

ISSN 1479-344X

ISBN 978 1 4654 6782 9

SPECIAL EDITIONS OF DK TRAVEL GUIDES

DK Travel Guides can be purchased
in bulk quantities at discounted prices
for use in promotions or as premiums.
We are also able to offer special
editions and personalized jackets,
corporate imprints, and excerpts from
all of our books, tailored specifically to
meet your own needs.

To find out more, please contact:

in the US
specialsales@dk.com

in the UK
travelguides@uk.dk.com

in Canada
specialmarkets@dk.com

in Australia
penguincorporatesales@
penguinrandomhouse.com.au